Branch Lines of
Gloucestershire

This engine, 0–4–2T No. 1401, was used in the film *The Titfield Thunderbolt*. Here it is at Berkeley Road with the 11.52 a.m. Berkeley Road to Lydney Town. It carries an 85B, Gloucester, Horton Road, shed plate.

14.6.58   R.E. Toop

Branch Lines of Gloucestershire

COLIN G. MAGGS

ALAN SUTTON

First published in the United Kingdom in 1991 by
Alan Sutton Publishing Ltd · Phoenix Mill · Stroud · Gloucestershire

First published in the United States of America in 1991 by
Alan Sutton Publishing Inc. · Wolfeboro Falls · NH 03896–0848

British Library Cataloguing in Publication Data

Maggs, Colin G.
Branch lines in Gloucestershire.
I. Title
385.094241

ISBN 0–86299–959–6

Library of Congress Cataloging in Publication Data applied for

Front cover: Collett 0–4–2T No. 1409 in unlined green livery, and auto coach W1668W at Sharpness, having arrived as the 4.55 p.m. from Berkeley Road on 20 July 1963 (Photograph: Hugh Ballantyne). Back cover: 2–6–2T No. 4100 hauling the 5.15 p.m. Kingham to Cheltenham train at Bourton-on-the-Water on 17 August 1962 (Photograph: Author).

Typeset in 9/10 Palatino.
Typesetting and origination by
Alan Sutton Publishing Limited.
Printed by The Bath Press, Bath, Avon.

Contents

Branch Lines of Gloucestershire

Introduction

The first line in the county was the nine-mile-long Bristol and Gloucestershire Railway opened in 1835 from Coalpit Heath. A purely mineral line, it was worked by horses, though approaching Bristol gravitation was used down an incline of 1 in 55. In 1835 a Bond and Winwood locomotive was tried, but unfortunately few details have survived – other than the fact that it exploded after being modified to make two trips daily instead of one.

With the development of railways, an extension to Gloucester was called for, and the 'shire' dropped from the company's title. Only twenty-one and a half miles of new line was needed as the Bristol and Gloucester Railway (BGR) planned to share Cheltenham and Great Western Union Railway (CGWUR) metals between Standish Junction and Gloucester. The opening of the BGR in 1844 completed the chain of rail communication between Newcastle-upon-Tyne and Exeter. It was also the first mixed gauge line in the country. As the Bristol and Gloucester was broad gauge, and the Avon and Gloucestershire Railway, which had running powers over the section between Coalpit Heath and Mangotsfield, standard gauge, the latter's rails were laid between those of the BGR. Furthermore, this length was particularly interesting as the AGR used horse traction, and the BGR steam locomotives. There was no risk of collision, however, as Major-General Pasley, the Board of Trade Inspecting Officer remarked that 'Railway trains drawn by horses seldom or never travel slower than the rate of 3 miles an hour. Hence as the Bristol & Gloucester Railway Company proposed to run six passenger trains on week-days, at intervals of not less than two hours and twenty minutes between succeeding trains, it is impossible that collision can take place, provided that the Avon & Gloucestershire Railway trains shall be so arranged as always to follow one of the Bristol & Gloucester passenger trains in a short time after the latter shall have passed on the junctions, whether travelling northwards or southwards.'

The line which carried passengers northwards from Gloucester was the Birmingham and Gloucester Railway. At first it was decided to take a direct route avoiding Droitwich, Worcester, Tewkesbury and Cheltenham, but residents of the latter town created such an uproar that the line was diverted to include it. The other towns had be be content with being served by a branch line. The line was opened between Gloucester and Camp Hill, Birmingham in 1840. In 1845 the Bristol and Birmingham companies were taken over by the Midland Railway (MR).

Closely allied with the Bristol and Gloucester was the Cheltenham and Great Western Union Railway. This left the London to Bristol main line at Swindon and cut through the Cotswolds to Stroud, Gloucester and Cheltenham, sharing, as mentioned above, its Standish to Gloucester length with the BGR, though in the event, as the CGWUR construction got behind schedule the BGR built this section. The Great Western Railway took over the CGWUR in 1844, completed the line and opened it to Gloucester in 1845 and onwards to Cheltenham two years later.

Gloucester had now become an important rail centre – significant in its own right as the chief town in the region, and also as a centre of routes due to its situation at the lowest point at which the River Severn could be conveniently crossed. The Severn railway bridge near Sharpness was not opened until 1879 and the tunnel in 1886.

The next main line in the county was the South Wales Railway (SWR) which carried trains from Gloucester to South Wales. Although nominally independent, it was entirely a Great Western project planned to work in conjunction with the line from Swindon. Although there was little opposition to the course of the line west of Newport, east of that town the route was disputed, some urging that the line be carried via Monmouth rather than follow a direct route along the coast. This debate delayed construction so that although the line from Chepstow to Swansea was opened in 1850, it was not until the following year that the line from Gloucester to Chepstow was ready. Even then the two sections of the SWR were not quite linked. Due to work on the bridge across the River Wye having fallen behind schedule, passengers from Gloucester were decanted at a temporary terminus a mile east of Chepstow and conveyed by road in horse buses to the permanent station on the west bank of the Wye. Through-running from Gloucester to South Wales eventually began in 1852.

The GWR cast covetous eyes at the Midland Railway's line between Gloucester and Birmingham and wondered whether it could take a share of this lucrative traffic. The Great Western already owned a line from Birmingham through Stratford-upon-Avon as far as Honeybourne, and towards the end of the nineteenth century traders and fruit growers of Broadway and Winchcombe pressed for a railway to serve their district. For the cost of a line a mere twenty and three-quarter miles in length between Honeybourne and Cheltenham, the GWR was able to create a new route to Birmingham. This opened throughout in 1906.

The line, the only main route in Gloucestershire not to have any branches, developed its potential in providing a direct Great Western route from Birmingham to Bristol and the West of England, and also South Wales, while apart from through trains, it generated a fair amount of traffic from the area particularly during the fruit-picking season. In the British Railways era it still continued to provide a parallel to the Gloucester to Birmingham route up the Lickey Incline. Then, following the derailment of a coal train which damaged the track at Winchcombe on 25 August 1976, it was considered uneconomic to repair and so the line was officially closed on 1 November 1976, since when it has been partially re-opened by the Gloucestershire Warwickshire Railway Society.

Although the inauguration of the South Wales line gave rail communication between South West England and South Wales, the route was hardly direct. As the crow flies Bristol is only twenty-five miles from Cardiff, but the rail route involved a distance of no less than ninety-three miles.

Technology in the 1840s was incapable of producing a suitable tunnel or bridge to reach the other side of the Severn, but a ferry was feasible. In 1858 construction of the Bristol and South Wales Union Railway (BSWUR) began from South Wales junction, a quarter of a mile east of Bristol Temple Meads, to New Passage Pier where paddle-steamers crossed two miles of water to Portskewett Pier. Here a short branch linked with the main SWR at Portskewett station. The BSWUR opened in 1863 and was the only main line in Gloucestershire, apart from that from Filton to Wootton Bassett, which did not serve the county town.

Although trains ran to the end of each pier, the route was no use for goods and mineral traffic, and unreliable for passengers as bad weather could bring the ferry to a halt. It is said that one nervous lady asked a seaman: 'Do people often drown on this crossing?' to which she received the reply, 'Only once ma'am, only once.'

It was Charles Richardson (who had also been responsible for building the Cheltenham and Great Western Union Railway), who when engaged on building the ferry piers, was led to consider constructing a tunnel under the Severn. In 1872 the Great Western obtained an Act to carry out his plan. Many problems had to be surmounted before it was eventually opened to goods traffic on 1 September 1886 and to local passenger trains three months later. London to South Wales expresses were not diverted through the tunnel, instead of via Gloucester, until 1 July 1887 by which time teething problems had been overcome.

Trains from South Wales to Swindon had to travel a rather circuitous route via Bristol and Bath, so a direct line was planned from Filton to Wootton Bassett. The railway was laid out for ease of running, no gradient being steeper than 1 in 300 and no curve sharper than one mile radius. Considering that the line had to cross the Cotswolds, this was a fine achievement. It opened in 1903.

The branch lines are described in the same order as the main lines which serve them.

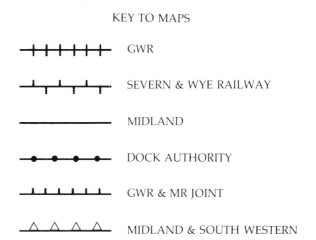

KEY TO MAPS

GWR

SEVERN & WYE RAILWAY

MIDLAND

DOCK AUTHORITY

GWR & MR JOINT

MIDLAND & SOUTH WESTERN

Avonside Wharf Branch, Bristol

This branch was the southern end of the Bristol and Gloucestershire Railway's main line. The horse tramway's terminus was at Cuckold's Pill, later called Avonside Wharf, on the Floating Harbour opposite what later became Temple Meads Station. When the coal tramway was turned into the Bristol and Gloucester Railway, a new main line was built from Lawrence Hill Junction to join the GWR just east of Temple Meads, the original line becoming a goods branch.

The Midland Railway took advantage of its Avonside Wharf and ran a fleet of nineteen 120-ton barges connecting the wharf with warehouses elsewhere in the city docks, and also transporting goods from the side of ships to Avonside Wharf either for storage, or to railway wagons. To assist the transfer of goods affected by weather, a covered dock 160 ft by 50 ft was provided. Avonside Goods Depot had extensive warehouses for the storage of flour, grain, cheese, sugar, tinned foods, dried fruit and other merchandise. Transfer at Avonside between water and land transport was eased by the provision of electric, steam and hydraulic cranes.

Quite divorced from rail access was the Midland Railway's King's Wharf, Redcliffe Street, where cellars hewn out of red sandstone were used for storing up to 8,000 barrels of non-inflammable oils, wax and so on, goods being carried to or from there by barge. The MR's red-painted fleet of barges was sold to Benjamin Perry & Son and George Head early in the twentieth century.

As was common at many goods sheds and depots, lack of space and sharp angles made points quite out of the question at some Avonside locations, so in such places wagon turntables were used to give access to sidings.

In the latter days of steam, wharf lines were shunted by ex-Lancashire and Yorkshire Railway 0–4–0ST 0F class 'pugs' Nos 51202 and 51212, while in diesel days, 03 class shunters were used.

In the 1950s traffic at the wharf included seed potatoes and goods for a sugar warehouse, Heinz food store, a paper works, a paint works, and Harvey's bottle store. The run-down of the depot began in the sixties, and by the early eighties only cement (and seasonally molasses for distillers) was dealt with, the former alone surviving until 1989.

The Avonside Wharf branch is interesting in that it changed its junction from one main line to another. This came about when the former Midland Railway line closed on 1 February 1970. To enable the wharf still to be used, a new chord line was opened from the GWR's Bristol to Filton line at Lawrence Hill.

Although the wharf itself is no longer open to traffic, part of the branch is still utilized. In the mid-eighties Avon County Council experienced refuse disposal problems and decided to send its rubbish by rail to a landfill site. Five days a week, a train is loaded with rubbish, compacted and placed in containers at Bath. It then proceeds down the wharf branch to the Great Western Refuse Transfer Station, Barrow Road, where more containers are loaded. It then moves on to Westerleigh for the final set of containers before proceeding to Calvert, Buckinghamshire where they are emptied.

An early locomotive builder, Henry Asprey Stothert, set up his business at Avonside Wharf, it being conveniently placed for receiving the raw materials required: coal brought by the Bristol and Gloucestershire Railway, and pig-iron arriving by sea. Stothert started in 1837, building engines for the GWR and Bristol and Exeter as well as other companies, turning out good work at low prices. During periods of recession, the firm diversified and manufactured marine engines, steam pumps and point capstans.

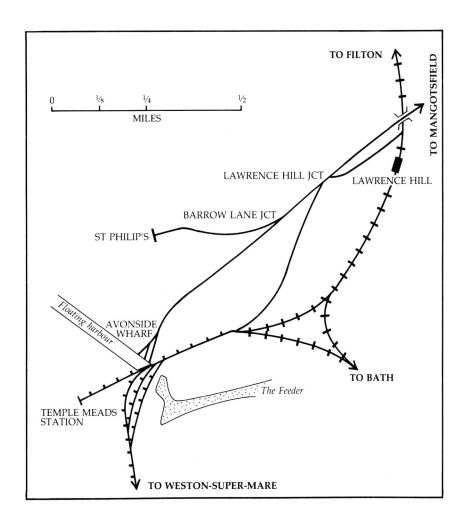

Avonside Wharf. Midland Railway barge No. 5 lies towards the centre of the picture. There are cranes on quayside for the transfer of goods between rail and water and covered goods depot for transfer of freight needing protection from weather is to the centre right.

1922   Author's Collection

An unusual sight – a passenger train on a goods-only branch. This was Railway Correspondence and Travel Society rail tour at Avonside Wharf. The view looks towards Lawrence Hill Junction. Notice that because of the sharp curve, the last coach is not in line with the one in front.

26.9.59   Dr A.J.G. Dickens

Mangotsfield to Bitton and the Branch to Westerleigh Rail Terminal

Although the Great Western Railway provided Bath with a good service to the east and west, a journey north involved a change at Bristol. This was a need which could be filled by building a branch from the main Midland Railway line at Mangotsfield. Another important advantage was that cheap coal could be brought to the city for domestic, industrial and gasworks use by way of this line.

Opened on 4 August 1869 and double-tracked from the beginning, the branch fulfilled its expectations, growing in importance when the Somerset and Dorset Railway was extended to Bath in 1874 making the Mangotsfield to Bath branch part of a north to south trunk artery. In 1944 it carried troops and supplies for the Normandy invasion and in the post-war era enjoyed particularly heavy passenger traffic on summer Saturdays.

Following the withdrawal of through north to south trains in 1962, the branch dealt principally with local traffic. Passenger services were withdrawn in 1966, though freight and mineral trains continued. The line was singled in May 1968 and following the closure of Bath gasworks after the introduction of North Sea gas, the branch closed on 31 May 1971. Some of the recovered track was re-laid on the Thornbury branch.

Branch stations in Gloucestershire were at Mangotsfield, Warmley, Oldland Common and Bitton. Mangotsfield station was at the apex of the junction of the lines to Gloucester and Bath from the Bristol direction. The platforms were covered by glazed roofs held by lightweight girders supported on slender cast-iron columns. The platforms were linked by a dark subway which inspired Arnold Ridley, the Bath author, to write *The Ghost Train*. It is said that when the subway was being excavated, the workmen undertaking the task were able to extract enough coal to boil water for their tea. Although principally a junction station used by passengers changing trains, there was a fair amount of local traffic, especially as the large Carson's chocolate factory was nearby.

Warmley station had buildings of timber construction, the waiting room on the 'Down' platform still remaining in occasional use as a café for users of the footpath and cycle track which today follows the course of the branch. On the far side of the level crossing site is the preserved signal-box. In its heyday, traffic at Warmley was considerable. In addition to dealing with general merchandise, a brick and pipe works which lay adjacent to the station provided sufficient traffic to fill three wagons weekly, while on alternate days, Douglas motor cycles arrived from the factory at Kingswood. However, the special traffic was ochre. It coloured the yard red. When wet it dyed boots and socks, but dry conditions were no better as it blew about and made the hair red. During the First World War coal was unofficially dug from the sides of the cuttings between Warmley and Bitton.

Oldland Common, opened on 2 December 1935, had sleeper-built platforms and was the only station on the branch to have electric lighting. During the severe winter of

1962–3, staffing leves were such that snow and ice could only be cleared from one end of the platform, so before arriving, the guard went through each train warning passengers to alight from the rear coach.

Bitton station is built of local stone to the typical Midland Railway two-pavilion design, but it was asymmetrical, having an extra office at the north end. In addition to general traffic, the station dealt with machinery and steel sheet, hides, market garden produce, chemicals, materials to and from a paper mill and moulding sand. At one period during the Second World War, two sets of coaches normally used on the Somerset and Dorset, were taken from Bath to Bitton each evening for storage in the goods yard. This procedure was carried out so that if the bridge outside Bath station had been bombed at night, the coaches would not have been trapped and thus been unavailable for use the next morning.

Bitton station is now the headquarters of the Avon Valley Railway which has re-laid and opened the length to Oldland Common and has plans for further extensions.

The Westerleigh branch has a very unusual history. It began life as part of the Bristol and Gloucester Railway's main line. As traffic developed, to ease congestion at Bristol, a marshalling yard was opened in 1900/1, eventually having thirteen roads on the 'Up' and twelve on the 'Down' side. During the Second World War these sidings were 'protected' by dummy wooden guns which, in fact, could not have been seen from the air, but reassured local civilians. With the closure of small stations and the consequent decrease in the amount of shunting required, the yards were taken out of service on 19 January 1965.

British Railways possessed two routes between Bristol and Yate: the BGR (later taken over by the Midland Railway) via Mangotsfield, and the GWR line via Filton. Modern signalling, plus a reduction of local passenger and freight traffic, meant that the Mangotsfield route could be closed, this taking place on 3 January 1970. Mangotsfield North junction to Bristol was closed completely, but the 'Down' main line from Yate South junction to Mangotsfield North junction was retained as a siding for training track machine operators, while the 'Up' main line between these points was used by coal trains to Bath gasworks. This latter use lasted only just over a year for these trains ceased in May 1971. The bridge built to carry the M4 Motorway over the line at what was the south end of Westerleigh Yard, was adapted for storing the track machines.

The line from Yate to Westerleigh received a new lease of life on 19 November 1985 when the first of Avon County Council's refuse transfer stations was opened on part of the former marshalling yard. Then in 1990, another part of the site, that between the refuse terminal and the M4, was developed as a Murco Petroleum terminal. The two sidings in this depot are of bull-head rail held on chairs on timber sleepers and are the property of Murco Petroleum.

Oil products arrive from Milford Haven by rail in 100-tonne tank cars, the depot being capable of handling a train thirty-two cars in length. The product is pumped from rail to one of seven storage tanks ready for delivery by road. A loop allows the locomotive to run round its train outside the Murco compound before it pushes the train into the two sidings, uncouples, and, to avoid any fire risk, then waits outside while the tanks are being discharged. On completion of this task, the locomotive re-enters the depot and returns the empties to Milford Haven. The inaugural train arrived on 1 March 1991. At the time of writing, three trains a week are expected, but it is hoped that this number will increase.

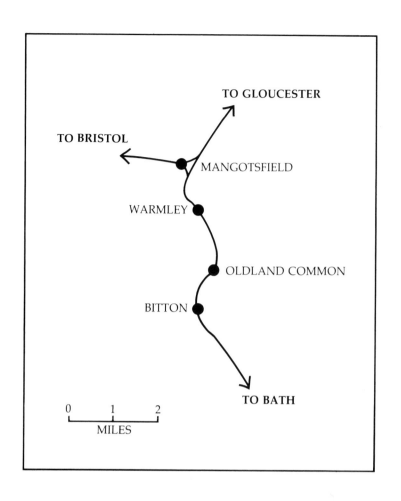

TO GLOUCESTER

TO BRISTOL

MANGOTSFIELD

WARMLEY

OLDLAND COMMON

BITTON

TO BATH

0   1   2
MILES

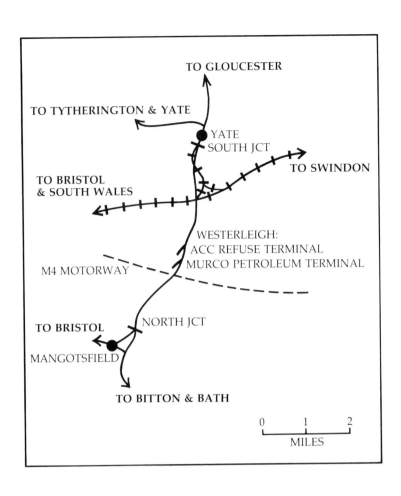

TO GLOUCESTER

TO TYTHERINGTON & YATE

YATE
SOUTH JCT

TO SWINDON

TO BRISTOL
& SOUTH WALES

WESTERLEIGH:
ACC REFUSE TERMINAL
MURCO PETROLEUM TERMINAL

M4 MOTORWAY

NORTH JCT

TO BRISTOL

MANGOTSFIELD

TO BITTON & BATH

0   1   2
MILES

BR Standard Class 3MT 2–6–2T No. 82036 at Mangotsfield with a Bristol Temple Meads to Bath Green Park stopping train. Notice the typical Midland Railway ridge and furrow roofs.

c. 1964   D. Payne

Warmley station looking towards Bitton. The timber-built waiting shelter, left, now used as a café, and the signal-box beyond the level crossing have been preserved.

c. 1905   M.J. Tozer Collection

Ex-Somerset and Dorset Railway Class 7F 2–8–0 No. 53806 working tender-first to Bath. The leading twenty or so wagons contain coal for Bath gasworks. A brick and tile works is to the right.
28.4.62   R.E. Toop

A unusual sight at Bitton – a farm removal train. Several cattle trucks are in evidence as are wagons for carrying farm machinery. One open wagon carries a container of furniture.
1933   Courtesy *Bath Evening Chronicle*

The Avon Valley Railway, Bitton, and Bristol-built Avonside 0–6–0ST *Edwin Hulse*.
8.5.76   Author

Bristol-built Peckett 0–6–0ST *Fonmon* passes the signal-box from Painswick Road crossing, Gloucester, which the preservationists have re-erected on the site of the former Bitton signal-box.
30.5.88   Author

Permanent way machine PW DX7 3414 at the northerly end of Westerleigh Yard. This is the view towards Yate.

1.3.91   Author

60033 *Anthony Ashley Cooper* testing track in the Murco oil distribution depot. This view was taken on the first occasion an engine had run over these lines.

1.3.91   Author

Yate to Thornbury

The first proposals for the branch were made in 1858 when it was planned to link collieries and ironstone fields at Frampton Cottrell and Iron Acton with the Midland Railway and Yate. Construction began in the mid-sixties and sufficient land was purchased for double track, but only single was ever laid. The branch opened to Frampton Cottrell in May 1868 and through to Tytherington by the following August. The principal engineering features, the 224 yd long Tytherington tunnel and the 167 yd long Grovesend tunnel, delayed completion of the line onwards to Thornbury until 2 September 1872. Unfortunately for the branch's economy, the mine at Frampton Cottrell closed in 1875. The terminus at Thornbury was built in stone to the typical twin pavilion MR station design of the period, but intermediate stations at Iron Acton and Tytherington were constructed of timber. The only signals on the branch were for protecting crossing gates.

The line was extra busy for a couple of weeks in 1885 when a whale became stranded in the River Severn at Littleton Pill. Using ropes and traction engines, the locals heaved it to the bank where in two weeks over 40, 000 visitors came to see it, many walking the four miles from the railhead at Thornbury.

Thornbury and the villages en route provided a certain amount of traffic, as did quarries in the Tytherington area. During the Second World War ambulance trains of twelve coaches worked through to Thornbury taking the wounded to hospital. The trains had to be divided in half in order to be brought alongside the platform which was not built for such a lengthy rake. Another interesting wartime feature was that when the LMS was short of locomotives, Southern Railway K10 class 4–4–0 No. 135 worked the branch goods trains.

In 1955 the plan to work sidings at Grovesend Quarry was for a train from Thornbury to back into the loop to pick up loaded ballast wagons and then draw forward at no more than 4 m.p.h. over an electric weighing machine which weighed the trucks as they passed slowly over it. As the heavy train was moving down a gradient of 1 in 64, it could not easily reverse to couple up to the brake van and any other trucks. Furthermore, the points were rather too near the mouth of Tytherington tunnel for the driver to see when the train was clear of them. To overcome these problems, a driver sometimes made an unofficial arrangement with the guard. The driver let the train of loaded ballast wagons slowly descend through the tunnel. The braking was assisted by some of the wagon brakes being pinned down. The train eventually stopped near Tytherington station to unpin the brakes and pick up the brake van and any other wagons which had descended by gravity behind the train. On one occasion a guard found he could not stop at Tytherington station and crashed into the train, causing his van to fall apart and injuring him sufficiently to require hospital treatment. Autumn was disliked by drivers as leaves on the Tytherington side of the tunnel made ascending the bank difficult. Snails could be found on a wall approaching the tunnel. One driver used to stick them on the upper part of the back of the fire-box and when cooked and ready for eating, prise them out with a safety pin.

The branch engine was stabled in a shed at Thornbury. There were two footplate crews – one on early and the other on late turn. Both firemen were in the 'Passed' grade so that in the event of a driver being sick, they could take over and be put in charge of a replacement firemen sent from Bristol. Visiting firemen tended to sleep in the porters' room at the station, thus saving lodging money and being on the spot for getting up early to prepare the engine. As it was a wooden engine shed, for safety reasons the fire had to be completely taken out before a locomotive was left. An engine never grew really cold overnight. Next morning the fireman just put a few fire-lighters in the fire-box and soon raised steam pressure before his driver booked on.

Water from a spring by Grovesend quarry ran through the tunnel to a tank at Thornbury which, as well as supplying the railway's needs, also supplied The Bathings – a cold water bathing pool owned by a small-holder to supplement his income. The same source also supplied the saw mills at Thornbury.

Passenger traffic was withdrawn on 19 June 1944, but goods continued until 4 December 1967 when the branch was closed, track lifting starting the following September. This was not to be the end of the story as, when Amalgamated Roadstone developed its Tytherington (Grovesend) quarry, it wanted a rail link. Fortunately this was no great problem. Six miles of track recovered from the Mangotsfield to Bath branch were relaid between Yate and Tytherington, the 20,000 tons of ballast required being supplied by the quarry. The branch re-opened on 3 July 1972. Some of the villagers complained that the track was noisy at night. The problem was solved by the joints being welded. Some limestone was taken over the re-opened branch to Avonmouth where it was exported. This was interesting as the quarry had supplied stone for the building there of the Royal Edward Dock. At the time of writing the branch is 'Out of service until further notice'.

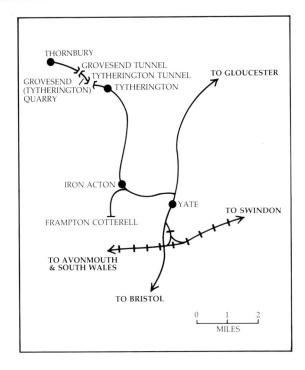

A rare view of a DMU on the Thornbury branch with both single-ended and double-ended cars at the Yate end of the line. It is believed that they were being used for driver training.

21.8.72   Author

'Peak' type 4 D192 having just crossed the Iron Acton bypass level crossing with a stone train.
14.9.73   W.H. Harbor

'Peak' type 4 D192 approaches Iron Acton level crossing. The roof of the former crossing keeper's cottage can be seen on the right.

14.9.73   W.H. Harbor

Class 4F 0–6–0 No. 44424 approaching Iron Acton station from Thornbury. Beyond the timber station building a chicken run has been built on the platform.

22.8.56 Author

Class 4F 0–6–0 No. 44424 climbing the gradient of 1 in 60 to Grovesend tunnel. The tower of Thornbury church can be seen on the right of the skyline.

22.8.56   Author

The author 'oiling' class 4F No. 44355 at Thornbury following a footplate ride from Yate.

17.8.56   Author

Class 1 0–4–4T No. 1388 at Thornbury with a train of four coaches. The paper boys carry *Bristol Times & Mirror* bags. The white-painted cattle pen appears in the background.

c. 1907   M.J. Tozer Collection

Horse-boxes galore as the Oldown Troop returns to Thornbury station. The Millenium Flour advertisement is flanked by posters advertising W&A Gilbey's wines and spirits.

c. 1907   M.J. Tozer Collection

Berkeley Road to Lydney

This branch was constructed by the Severn Bridge Railway to link the Severn and Wye Railway and the GWR at Lydney, with the Midland Railway at Berkeley Road, giving the MR valuable access to the Forest of Dean. The branch enabled ships which had unloaded at Sharpness to coal there and thus avoid the expense of sailing to a South Wales port.

The line's principal feature was the 4,162 ft long Severn Bridge, the longest English railway bridge, and in the British Isles, third only to those spanning the Tay and Forth. It was a series of iron bow-string girders resting on cast-iron piers filled with concrete and rock. At its eastern end was a steam-operated swing span across the Gloucester and Berkeley Canal. An engine driver was required to be on duty on one of the day shifts in order to keep the engine and machinery in good order, the signalman on the the other shift assisting in cleaning and coaling. The swing span was left open to shipping at night and also at other times when the railway was not in use, the man on early turn being required to have the engine in steam ready for swinging the span at least twenty minutes before the first train was due. The man on late turn was responsible for banking the fire after the last train had passed and the swing span was opened. The two boilers were used alternately for a fortnight; one being in use while the other was being washed out.

The bridge was opened to traffic on 17 October 1879, curiously enough exactly a century after the first iron bridge in the world was constructed, which was also built across the Severn. To reimburse the cost of the bridge, the railway company was allowed to charge a bonus of three additional miles.

The opening of the Severn tunnel in 1886 somewhat eclipsed the bridge, but on winter Sundays when the Civil Engineer had complete possession of the tunnel, trains were diverted across the bridge. The largest engines permitted to cross the bridge were Dean goods and so this class was not scrapped so quickly as it might have been in order to have engines to haul Bristol to South Wales trains when the tunnel was closed. Later 43XX class 2–6–0s were authorized to run, allowing the Dean goods to be withdrawn.

When Portskewett Pier caught fire in May 1881 and the ferry to Old Passage was temporarily cancelled, passengers from Bristol to South Wales travelled via the bridge. This alternative route proved to be twenty-five minutes quicker, but, nevertheless following temporary repairs, the ferry was put back into operation.

The Severn Bridge Railway failed to prosper, fell into Chancery in 1883 and two years later was sold to the GWR and MR, which, together with the latter's branch from Berkeley Road to Sharpness, opened on 1 August 1876, and became part of the Severn and Wye joint line. The locomotive department came under the supervision of the GWR, while the MR undertook line maintenance, passenger coaches being supplied equally by the two companies. In 1931, to effect an economy, the line between Berkeley Road and Sharpness was singled.

Between the wars, the Great Western wanted to use the bridge as an alternative to the tunnel and wished to try heavier locomotives but the LMS, as successor to the Midland, would not allow this. Soon after the Second World War when the line fell into the hands of British Railways' Western Region completely, this Derby regulation was abolished and heavier engines were permitted.

During the Second World War, it was not unknown for pilots on training flights to dive Spitfires and Hurricanes between the bridge deck and the water. An onlooker admired them, until he saw men painting the bridge, hanging in their cradle while an aircraft flew within a few feet of them.

The bridge's death blow came on the night of 25 October 1960 when it was struck by an oil tanker and two spans were destroyed. If this tragic accident had not occurred, the line would probably still be open, as new track had been laid across the bridge, and Fairfield's of Chepstow were more than three-quarters of their way through a contract for strengthening the bridge in order to allow even heavier engines to use it for a least a further fifty years. However, when BR was faced with a bill of £294,000 for replacing the broken spans, it was decided that repair could not be justified.

Unfortunately for BR, under the Merchant Shipping Act, the limited liability for damage through collision did not exceed the sum equal to about twenty-four times the net registered tonnage of the vessel, or vessels. BR only received £5,000, while Fairfield's, which lost plant to the value of £10,000, received just a little over £100.

BR took more than six years to make up its mind what to do with the bridge, but in 1967 arranged with the Nordman Construction Company of Gloucester to dismantle and remove the bridge and masonry approach arches, the spans being used to form a road bridge in Chile. It was probably a wise decision to get rid of the structure, as it had been struck by shipping no less than seven times between 1939 and 1961. At half tide the water rushed past the piers in a ten-knot millrace and if a vessel had struck the bridge at this speed just as a passenger train was crossing, the results would have been unthinkable.

After the collapse of the two spans, the Lydney end of the branch was closed completely, trains only running between Berkeley Road and Sharpness. Passenger services were withdrawn on 2 November 1964, but the branch still remains open for freight and at the time of writing about two trains a week leave Berkeley carrying nuclear flasks containing spent elements from Berkeley Power Station.

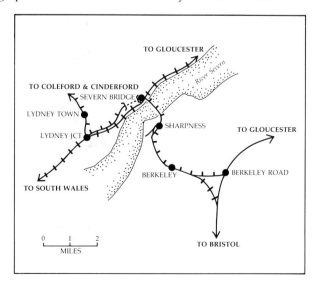

'Berkeley Road change for Sharpness' nameboard. 'Lydney' has been pasted over, damage to the Severn bridge having curtailed the service.

1964   D. Payne

Berkeley Road: 'Peak' class D99 with steam leaking from its steam heating pipes, is working the 7.45 a.m. Bristol to Sheffield. On the right, 0–4–2T No. 1453 is in charge of the 8.15 a.m. to Sharpness on the last day of the branch's passenger service.

31.10.64   Hugh Ballantyne

Class 4F 0–6–0 No. 44264 heading an 'Up' goods, about to leave the Sharpness branch at Berkeley Road.

11.5.61   Author

Type 1 diesel-hydraulic D9522 climbing out of Sharpness with the 1.20 p.m. freight.

1.6.67   Author

In unhappy condition near the end of its service 0–4–2T No. 1453 at Sharpness with a painted smoke box number-plate in place of a cast-iron one. It is hauling auto trailer W244W. This has an all-steel body and was built in 1953. The train is the 4.15 p.m. to Berkeley Road.

26.9.64   Hugh Ballantyne

A Ford Consul crossing the high level road/rail swing bridge at Sharpness docks.

22.8.56   Author

The swing span of the Severn bridge, with a view towards Lydney, and the Gloucester and Berkeley Canal in the foreground.

Author's Collection

Erecting the main spans of the Severn bridge.

October 1879   Courtesy *Engineering*

A rare sight; No. 5959 *Mawley Hall* and No. 5042 *Winchester Castle* testing the Severn bridge.
17.7.56   Author's Collection

The view from near Severn bridge station towards Sharpness.

c. 1905   Author's Collection

A notice which stood beside the Gloucester and Berkeley Canal just south of the Severn Bridge.
1964   D. Payne

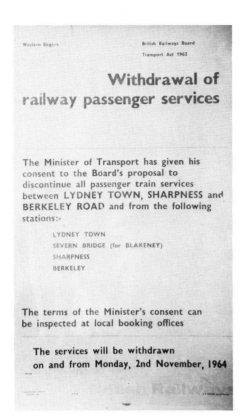

Withdrawal of railway passenger services

The Minister of Transport has given his consent to the Board's proposal to discontinue all passenger train services between LYDNEY TOWN, SHARPNESS and BERKELEY ROAD and from the following stations:-

LYDNEY TOWN
SEVERN BRIDGE (for BLAKENEY)
SHARPNESS
BERKELEY

The terms of the Minister's consent can be inspected at local booking offices

**The services will be withdrawn
on and from Monday, 2nd November, 1964**

The closure notice posted at Berkeley station.
September 1964   D. Payne

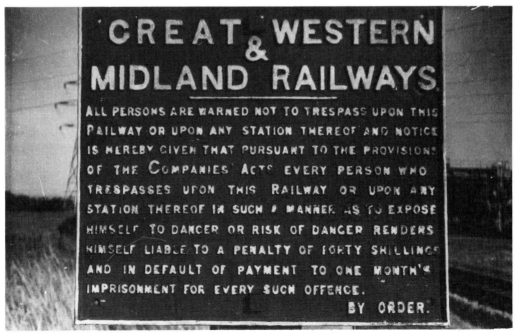

A notice at Berkeley station.

September 1964   D. Payne

The signalman at Severn bridge signal-box about to hand the single-line tablet to the fireman of No. 1627. The signal-box, of Midland Railway type, has replaced that shown on p. 29.

19.7.58   R.E. Toop

A Severn bridge tunnel notice preserved at the Dean Forest Railway, Norchard.

Author

An animated scene at Lydney Junction, Severn and Wye platforms. Engine 0–4–2T No. 1401 with the 11.52 a.m. Berkeley Road to Lydney Town is having its tanks filled.

14.6.58   R.E. Toop

Coaley to Dursley

Due to engineering difficulties, the Bristol and Gloucester Railway could not serve Dursley, but held to the flatter country nearer the Severn. This was far from satisfactory for mill owners of the Cam valley who saw their rivals in the Stroud area prosper through having canal and rail transport to bring fuel and raw materials and also carry away the finished product. Discussions led to a company being set up to build a line from the town to the main line at Coaley. The concern was far from prosperous and most unusually, the directors and secretary were all unpaid. Unable to afford new rails and chairs, the company obtained second-hand material from the Midland Railway which had by now taken over the BGR. The Dursley and Midland Junction Railway was opened to goods traffic on 25 August 1856 and to passengers on the 17th of the following month, the line being worked by the Midland.

A year later, the company with its finances £1,000 in the red, decided it could operate the line more economically itself. Surprisingly, the small tank engine used by H.D. Yeatman of Gloucester, the contractor who built the line, was still there, probably parked on length of spare track. It was offered for sale at £612, but after bargaining, the company managed to secure it for £434 10s. 0d. It had been built at Bristol, probably by Stothert, Slaughter and Company in the 1840s. Passengers were carried in two four-wheeled coaches borrowed from the Midland, but these were far from the latest thing in comfort. The new arrangements did not lead to any dramatic improvements in the line's profitability and the financial situation grew worse. This resulted in the MR purchasing the line in 1860, Dursley shareholders losing £11 10s. 0d. on every £20 share.

The junction station at Coaley was built in cottage style, with its buildings curiously set at right angles to the main line. The bridge over the River Cam, originally of timber, was replaced in concrete in 1948 after the ganger had refused to accept responsibility for it when he observed it moving beneath trains.

Unusually, the locomotive shed at Dursley actually pre-dated the railway, it being an existing structure converted to this new use. This shed being towards the far end of the branch meant that if a relief fireman was required from Gloucester, he had to travel from his home shed to Coaley junction by goods train, arriving there about midnight. Then he was faced with a walk in the dark up to Dursley where he lit the fire in the engine and raised steam for the first passenger train. During the day there was little rest for him as the small fire-box quickly became full of ash and clinker, so when the engine was not actually running, he either had to clean the fire, or fill the tanks with water. In 1884 the water supply for the engine was assured by a payment of £50 to Colonel Graham 'for a perpetual supply of water to the Dursley Locomotive Tank'.

In more recent times, passenger trains consisted of one coach, hauled, until 1957, by an ancient Midland tank engine with no back to the cab, so that when the engine was in reverse, as it was for half of its running life, the head and shoulders of the driver and fireman were exposed to the elements. These locomotives were known to the crews as

'Get wets'. In 1957 the branch came under the aegis of BR Western Region, and GWR-type tank engines were used of a modern design dating only from 1949. Trains for the last few months of the passenger service were worked by a relatively large tender engine which looked rather extravagant heading a one coach train. The branch passenger service was withdrawn on 10 September 1962, but goods trains serving the various private sidings still continued. General freight traffic finished on 1 November 1966 and with the closure of Messrs R.A. Lister's private siding, the branch finally shut on 13 July 1970. The level crossing gates from Coaley Road and Cam are in the care of the Dean Forest Railway Society at their Norchard Steam Centre. This is a curious coincidence, for at one time the former Severn and Wye Railway tank engine *Sabrina*, taken over by the Midland Railway, actually ran over the Dursley branch.

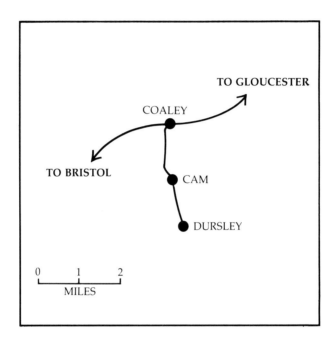

The destination board which was attached to the branch coach showed 'Dursley' on one side and 'Coaley Jn' on the reverse.

Author

0–4–2T No. 202 at Dursley station.

c. 1865   Author's Collection

Running tender-first, class 2MT 2–6–0 No, 46526 approaches Coaley with the 4.15 p.m. ex-Dursley.

13.6.62   Author

Class 1F 0–6–0T No. 41748 about to cross the partly-timber Quag bridge with an 'Up' goods train.
c. 1954   M.E.J. Deane

Class 1F 0–6–0T No. 41748 shunting at Dursley. Notice the open back to the cab.

c. 1954   M.E.J. Deane

Class 2F 0–6–0 No. 58165 (22B, Gloucester) shunting at Dursley.

c. 1954   M.E.J. Deane

Class 1F 0–6–0T No. 41720 (22B, Gloucester) at Dursley.

25.8.56   M.E.J. Deane

Class 1F 0–6–0T No. 41720 at Dursley shed. Notice the open-backed cab.

c. 1954   M.E.J. Deane

Class 2F 0–6–0 No. 58206 at Dursley with the 8.15 p.m. to Coaley. Notice the briquettes in the tender.

7.5.55   R.E. Toop

Type 1 diesel-hydraulic D9517 shunting at Dursley. Although the yard is busy, the permanent way shows signs of neglect.

1.6.67   Author

Stonehouse to Stroud and Nailsworth

By the mid-nineteenth century, as Nailsworth was still only served by road, mill owners there felt a strong need for a railway and set up a steering committee. Opposition by the Stroudwater Canal Company was placated by offering a free transhipment siding at Stonehouse wharf. The canal's manager advocated transferring railway wagons to pontoons at this wharf and then floating them to wharfs and mills, but this interesting proposal never came into being.

The plan put forward in 1854 for building a line to Nailsworth was rejected by the Parliamentary Committee, partly due to religious prejudice, a concept rarely figuring in railway schemes. One member of the committee said, 'I should have supported this Bill, only I find it would give greater facilities for attending a certain Roman Catholic chapel at Woodchester, and as I have pledged myself to resist the Pope, the devil and all his works, individually and collectively, I agree with the last two speakers' – these were against the line.

The company eventually obtained its Act in 1863 and the task of construction began. The excavation of the line certainly caused one householder problems. A sliding clay slope made the foundations of a house slip and forced its occupier to take to bed with him the necessary tools to open his bedroom door each morning.

The branch eventually opened to goods traffic on 1 February 1867 and to passengers three days later. Like the Dursley line, the company was financially unsound, so became part of the Midland Railway's empire in 1878. Ambitious plans were made to extend the line through Tetbury and Malmesbury to the Great Western's Bristol to London route and also onwards to a junction with the London and South Western Railway near Salisbury. The proposesd scheme left its mark at Nailsworth where the passenger station was built on an embankment above the goods yard in a postion where it would have been easier for a line to have climbed over the Cotswolds.

The spur from Dudbridge to Stroud came about as a result of the Great Western using broad gauge track. Stroud mill owners found the necessity for goods to be transhipped to another gauge at Gloucester frustrating. For example, John Hunt, owner of two large cloth factories, said that his wool came from Hull and if a standard gauge line was built to Stroud, his wool could be carried throughout by the Midland Railway. The branch proved highly expensive to construct – £37,198 for one and a quarter miles, whereas many lines cost less than £10,000 a mile. The Midland Railway's extension to Stroud was opened to goods on 16 November 1885 and to passengers on 1 July 1886.

The Nailsworth and Stroud branches were early sufferers from motor bus competition, Jeffery & Co. of Nailsworth starting a service in April 1908 undercutting railway fares.

The decision to close the branches to passenger traffic from 16 June 1947 was made on the government's instruction for a reduction in passenger mileage under a fuel economy campaign designed to help counteract a serious post-war fuel shortage. It was stated that it was not a permanent suspension, though the local press was informed that it would be for 'at least during the summer months'. Then on 8 June 1949 it was announced that passenger closure would be permanent.

Goods trains continued to run to Stroud and Nailsworth – the latter line having no less than five private sidings serving factories away from stations. Timber came by rail from Sharpness docks to Stroud but this traffic was lost to road about 1962 when the railway raised its tariff, ironically lorries being off-loaded on to land rented from BR. The last freight train ran on 1 June 1966, the track being lifted the following year. This was not quite the end of the story, for subsequently much of the formation has been turned into a walkway and cycle track.

The stations at Ryeford, Dudbridge and Nailsworth had quite imposing buildings in Cotswold stone, that at Nailsworth being particularly impressive as befitted the headquarters of the Stroud and Nailsworth Railway. Woodchester station, opened as an afterthought, was curious in that it had creosoted, instead of painted, timber. The ladies' waiting room alone had an open fire and so was used by all in winter, regardless of sex.

It was considered an 'old man's branch' since no fast work was called for and no night duty required. It was, therefore, ideal for drivers nearing retirement and for whom trips on the main line might prove too strenuous. On the other hand, duties being relatively light, the firemen on the branch were often young, so youth and age were seen together on the footplate.

Train crews had their quirks. Charlie 'Cuckoo' Hickman was excellent at imitating the bird which gave him his nickname and often fooled passengers. One old passenger-guard kept on during the Second World War long past retiring age, always endeavoured to find an excuse to avoid uncoupling an engine when it had to run round its train at the end of a journey. He used the ploy of trying to be seen busily occupied at such moments: assisting with luggage, or telling passengers the time of a connecting train, so that the fireman had to cope with uncoupling and coupling alone. On one occasion this guard did jump down on to the permanent way at Nailsworth to couple up and then was distracted by a lady talking to him. He then climbed back on the platform, and in due course, waved his flag and the train set off. When the driver arrived at Woodchester he found to his mortification that there were no coaches – the guard had forgotten to couple up.

Locomotive crews received various 'perks'. Bean sticks could be cut from the lineside at Nailsworth and Dudbridge. Rather less honestly, one driver kicked off coal near Dudbridge and was rewarded with a box of eggs; another driver performing the same trick near a public house was rewarded with a pint. Logs could be bought cheaply from the timber mill at Ryeford and carried back on the locomotive's footplate for domestic burning. A train sometimes stopped at Whiting's Crossing, just short of the branch platform at Stonehouse, for the driver to take a rabbit from a snare he had set earlier in the day.

As well as daytime excursions to Weston-Super-Mare, some to that destination ran in the evening. Leaving about 5.30 p.m. trippers had about four hours at the seaside, arriving back in Nailsworth around midnight. One day trip was run from Nailsworth to Paris, though no doubt the return trip was overnight. It must have been a memorable and exciting outing.

On an excursion to Portsmouth, four passengers returned very late at Stonehouse after the last branch train had gone. Asking the station-master what they should do, they received the reply 'walk'. Saying that as they had bought a return ticket they considered it the railway's duty to return them to Nailsworth, the station-master rang

Class 1P 0–4–4T No. 1390 at Stonehouse on the last day of the regular passenger service on the branch. The driver, right of the boy on the cab footstep, is Charlie 'Cuckoo' Hickman.

14.6.47   Author's Collection

Class 3F 0–6–0 No. 43754 between Stonehouse and Ryeford.

31.5.56   Author

A special train carrying a GEC transformer to the Midlands Electricity Board sub-station at Ryeford.

29.3.65   D. Payne

Class 1P 0–4–4T No. 1330 entering Ryeford from Dudbridge. Notice the wide platform.
28.5.47   R.J. Buckley

Class 3F 0–6–0 No. 43754 passing Woodchester station en route to Nailsworth.

31.5.56   Author

0–4–4T No. 1730 (re-numbered No. 1323 in 1907) having run through the stop blocks at Nailsworth. The passenger coach became detached from its bogie and felled the locomotive's chimney.

Author's Collection

Class 3F 0–6–0 No. 43754 (22B, Gloucester) taking water at Nailsworth. Notice the brazier to the right of the tender. This was lit in cold weather to prevent the water freezing.

31.5.56   Author

RAILWAY PLANT.

Stonehouse and Nailsworth Railway,
Stonehouse Station, Gloucester.

Re Contract Corporation Company, Limited.

BY ORDER OF THE OFFICIAL LIQUIDATOR,

Mr. WILLIAM FREEMAN,

(Proprietor of "Aldridges," St. Martin's Lane, London,)

WILL SELL BY PUBLIC AUCTION,

WITHOUT RESERVE,

ON TUESDAY, JUNE 18th, 1867, at 12 o'clock, at
STONEHOUSE STATION,—

THE whole of the CONTRACTOR'S PLANT,
which has been used in the construction of the
Stonehouse and Nailsworth Railway, consisting of a

POWERFUL CYLINDER TANK LOCOMOTIVE;

SMALL PILE ENGINE AND MONKEY;

53 END TIP WAGGONS;

A LARGE QUANTITY of TEMPORARY RAILS;

TRAVELLING CRANE;

Twelve dobbin carts; hand and wheelbarrows; a
number of permanent sleepers; many thousand feet
lineal of planking; platelayer's levers; timber and
stone drags; single and double-purchase crabs;
portable forge; sheriff and pinch bars; a large quantity
of chairs; fish plates; fang and fish bolts; temporary
and permanent crossing blocks; cast-iron barrow
wheels; round, twisted and square spikes; wrought
and cut nails; drag; tip and dobbin chains; earth
pick and beaters' heads; ratchet braces; screw jacks;
taps and dies; many lots of quarry and plate-laying
implements; scrap iron; and sundry other effects.

The lots may be viewed Two Days before the Sale,
and Catalogues had of C. F. Kemp, Esq., the Official
Liquidator, 8, Walbrook; Messrs. Linklater and Co.,
7, Walbrook; M. Abrahams, Esq., 8, Old Jewry,
London; on the Premises at Stonehouse Station; and
of Mr. Wm. Freeman, "Aldridge's," St. Martin's
Lane, London.

An advert in the *Stroud Journal*, 8 June 1867.

Stroud and Nailsworth Railway seal in Stroud
Museum.

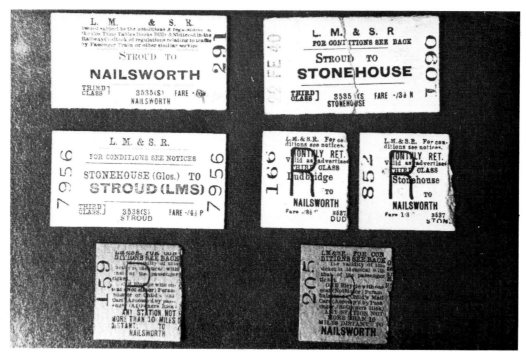

A selection of branch tickets.

Branch train staffs, front to rear: Dudbridge Junction–Stroud, Dudbridge Junction–Nailsworth, Stonehouse–Dudbridge Junction.

Gloucester
New Docks, High Orchard and Llanthony Docks Branches

The Midland Railway owned extensive lines serving Gloucester docks on the Gloucester and Berkeley Ship Canal. The variously named New Docks, Tuffley, or Hempsted branch ran from Tuffley Junction (where the hitherto parallel MR and GWR divided to make their separate ways to Gloucester), to Hempsted Wharf. The branch opened to goods on 24 May 1900, a sub-branch, opened in 1913, served the gasworks. Another line crossed Monk Meadow where, until 1938, it linked with the GWR's docks line. At Monk Meadow a dock and large pond for floating timber had been constructed west of the canal in 1891 and 1896 respectively. In 1969 the branch closed west of the gasworks siding and was shut completely two years later.

The dock at High Orchard was cut for the Birmingham and Gloucester Railway about 1840, the railway erecting coke ovens in its yard by the dock. Early locomotives burned coke rather than coal, this producing practically no smoke. In January 1843 one shareholder criticized the dock saying it was 'so ingeniously constructed as to be fed by a stream of water which is fast filling it up with mud, and so admirably situated as to be inaccessible. The presumption would be that this is a receptacle intended for traffic, and that it will be surrounded by sheds and warehouses for the reception of goods; but the only buildings contiguous are six large coke ovens, which are not at work because the coke could be contracted for elsewhere on better terms. The wet basin is a melancholy spectacle; especially when it is considered that at the bottom of its foul waters lie something like £14,000 of our money.'

The Birmingham and Gloucester Railway opened a 250 yd long spur from its Gloucester station to the horse-worked Gloucester and Cheltenham tramway in order that goods could be carried from the docks in standard gauge wagons. This traffic was considerable, no less than 45,000 tons being carried in 1845. However, the tramway was not suitable for all traffic – for instance 5,000 long baulks of timber had to be carried through the streets as they were incapable of negotiating the tramway's sharp curves. The obvious solution was to build a standard gauge line to the docks. Although the branch was not fully opened until 1848, certainly the portion from Barton Street level crossing to Rignum Place was in use by mid-September 1847 as it was the scene of a tragic accident. Horses drew wagons from the docks to Rignum Place where a locomotive completed haulage to the goods station. The engine was not fitted with an ash box and dropped live cinders on the line, which for years had been used as a footpath. Ann Williams, aged six, played with some of these embers and while doing so, another cinder behind her set fire to her frock causing fatal injuries.

Thomas Knowles, Locomotive Superintendent at Gloucester, gave details of the line's working at the inquest. The locomotive used the branch between four and twelve times daily, one man riding on the front buffer and another travelling behind on a low truck coupled to the engine. It was the men's duty to keep children from following or getting in the way of the engine. If the locomotive failed to clear all the wagons from the road at Rignum Place by 7 p.m., the time the dock gates closed, the engine made a further trip, but using lights, one lamp being fixed to the engine and the two men carrying a lamp in their hands. The man in front dismounted before Barton Street crossing and signalled if the line was clear. The engine could be stopped in an average distance of twelve yards, and sometimes in four or five yards.

Following the completion of the High Orchard branch, the MR filled in High Orchard dock to form a goods yard. Most of the lines around the docks were owned by the dock company and were authorized to be worked by the GWR and MR jointly. The dock company's line connected with both main line companies' metals via Llanthony Road swing bridge which carried both road and railway over the canal. The MR lines were on the eastern side of the canal.

The High Orchard branch left the main line at Barton Street junction, and divided west of Southgate Street level crossing, one line carrying straight on to High Orchard, while the other curved northwards to serve the old docks. There lines served many industrial firms, mostly connected with the import/export trade. One important company was the Gloucester Railway Carriage and Wagon Works. The High Orchard line was closed on 1 October 1971.

A broad gauge branch from Over Junction trailing off to Llanthony Docks on the Gloucester and Berkeley Canal opened on 20 March 1854. It had no less than three bridges: 68 yd, 37 yd and 99 yd in length respectively. Behind the quay, the GWR created a goods yard. Traffic developed and in the mid-1860s the canal company built transit sheds to store imported grain awaiting transfer to the railway, while additionally, the GWR provided shed and mobile steam cranes.

The Llanthony Docks branch also served Castle Meads power station, a small, coal-fired concern opened on 2 September 1941 and finally closed in 1977. The power station sidings were shunted by a fireless Andrew Barclay 0–4–0 built in 1942 and last used by the Central Electricity Generating Board in 1969.

Over the last twenty years the docks branch has seen decreasing use, regular traffic ceasing early in 1989. This was for the Blue Circle Cement Depot located in Llanthony Yard and normally trip-worked by a class 08 shunter from Gloucester New Yard.

Class 0F 0–4–0T No. 41537 shunting near Southgate Street level crossing at the junction of High Orchard and the docks branches.

14.4.60 Author

Metropolitan-Cammell three-car DMU M50338/M59115/M50304 stands at High Orchard with a rail tour from Birmingham. The unit had previously visited the Llanthony Docks line only some 50 yd distant as the crow flies, but taking forty minutes travelling time to circumnavigate the city.

21.11.70 Hugh Ballantyne

Hempsted Wharf sidings – the view towards the Gloucester and Berkeley Canal. Parallel with the branch's main line is a loop siding to the right, and three loop sidings to the left. The siding branching off to the left leads to the gasworks. Standing on the right is the hut containing the ground frame. To the right of this hut is a chemical works served by a siding. The contractors' wagons, left, have their axle boxes covered to prevent foreign bodies entering. The rail-built stop block on the far left is sturdily constructed.

c. 1914   Author's Collection

A train is hauled by 08836 over the River Severn viaduct.

29.8.85   Author

stop at Tewkesbury station, crossed the High Street and went down the Quay branch, fortunately coming under control before plunging into the river. The excitements of the race course must have seemed quite tame after this adventure.

Apart from this mishap, locomotive working proved a success, so the writing was on the wall for Trotman who was no longer required to provide horse power after 18 February 1844 except for making a connection with the Night Mail, the engine being serviced at this hour.

The original station in High Street was closed on 16 May 1864 when the MR extended the line from Tewkesbury to the GWR at Great Malvern, a station being opened on this new line.

With increasing competition from road transport, weekday passenger services were cut back to Upton-on-Severn in 1952, passenger trains continuing to run on the remaining section until 14 August 1961. The Quay branch had been closed on 1 February 1957. The engine shed at Tewkesbury remained in use until 7 September 1962 and the line between Ashchurch and Tewkesbury completely closed on 2 November the same year.

Ashchurch was an interesting station. W-shape in plan, the main line was served by two platforms, while the Tewkesbury and Evesham branches had but one each. At the north end of the station, a direct line from Tewkesbury to Evesham crossed the main line on the level at right angles.

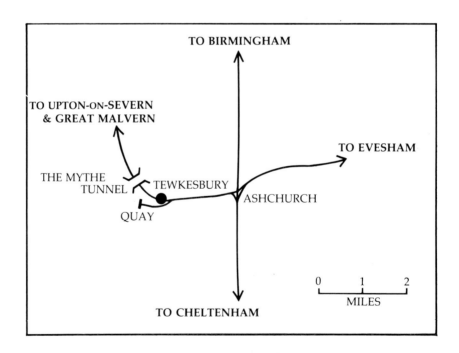

The direct line from Tewkesbury to Evesham crosses the Birmingham to Gloucester main line from left to right on the level. No. 45602 *British Honduras* approaches with the 12.30 p.m. York to Bristol express.

9.7.55   Hugh Ballantyne

Ashchurch station, the Tewkesbury branch platform.

Lens of Sutton

Class 3F 0–6–0 No. 43645 (22B, Gloucester) at Tewkesbury locomotive shed.

16.5.57   Hugh Ballantyne

Gloucester's Class 3F 0–6–0 No. 43754 and solitary brake third M21026M, leaving the Mythe, or Tewkesbury, tunnel on a rising 1 in 278 gradient. The train is the 5.10 p.m. Ashchurch to Upton-on-Severn. The right-hand line was retained for wagon storage.

16.5.57   Hugh Ballantyne

Kemble to Cirencester

When the Cheltenham and Great Western Union Railway opened to Cirencester on 31 May 1841, the town found that it temporarily had the railway's main station, instead of being located at the end of a branch. This state of affairs lasted for four years until 12 May 1845 when the Kemble to Standish line was completed allowing trains to reach Gloucester via Bristol and Gloucester Railway metals.

At first, the station at Kemble was merely a set of platforms for allowing a change of train and with no public access from outside. The station for the district was at Tetbury Road on the far side of the Fosse Way. This situation arose because Squire Robert Gordon, Secretary to the Treasury, would not permit a public station to be built on his land. Thus Kemble did not appear in the public timetable until 1872.

About a year after the branch opened, driver Jim Hurst was accused of the serious offence of carrying passengers on his locomotive from Cirencester to Kemble and not handing the fares to the company. Required to answer this charge in person before the directors in the boardroom at Paddington, Hurst was able to produce a letter from the joyriders certifying that while he did give two friends a ride contrary to the company's regulations, he neither asked for, nor received any money. He was very fortunate to receive only a reprimand.

To reduce the costs of working the branch, on 2 February 1959 trains were replaced by a railbus, a startling innovation and the first on the Western Region of British Railways. Shorter than a conventional railcar, it ran on four, rather than eight, wheels though seating forty-six passengers and allowing space for luggage. These railbuses ran a more intensive service than the steam trains they replaced and also served a new halt opened at Chesterton Lane. To keep costs as low as possible, the platform was at rail level like those on the continent, rather than at the floor level of the railbus as is standard practice in Britain. This new halt proved popular and encouraged BR to open a halt at Park Leaze.

It was the original intention to run the railbuses through to Swindon to obviate the tiresome change at Kemble, but this proved impossible as the lightweight railbus could not be relied upon to operate the signalling track circuits on the main line. As this was considered a hazard, they were not allowed to carry passengers when travelling on the main line. Another disadvantage of the railbus was that it sometimes suffered through overcrowding, but this had to be tolerated as replacement with a larger railcar would have increased operating costs and interfered with the cyclic working in conjunction with the Tetbury branch. These railbuses carried the first conductor-guards to work on BR – another economy since it meant that there was no need for booking clerks and ticket collectors at stations. Despite the fact that the branch received considerable support from the locality, it was declared uneconomic and closed to passengers on 6 April 1964, goods traffic being withdrawn eighteen months later.

Cirencester station, designed by I.K. Brunel and his residential assistant, R.P.

Brereton, is a good example of Victorian Gothic railway architecture carried out in stone. Originally built with a small overall roof, this train shed was removed in 1874. However, the standard platform canopy replacing it did not give the required balance and made the building appear tall and narrow when viewed from the ends. In 1956 a partial rebuilding took place, H.E.B. Cavanagh taking great care to maintain the original style.

The present Kemble station is the outcome of a Great Western director having a cold wait at the junction. Six acres of land were bought for £1,650 in 1881, an agreement being made with Miss Anna Gordon, who had inherited the property following the decease of the Squire, that no intoxicating liquor would be sold on the premises and the only houses built would be for employees. This resulted in the construction of a terrace together with detached homes for the station-master and an inspector. Today's station, with its mock Tudor design harking back to the railway style of forty years before, was built in 1882 by Griffith Griffiths for £4,850. With its latest re-paint, the barley-sugar-stick-shaped cast-iron supports carrying the platform canopy have their capitals imaginatively coloured – yellow daffodils and green leaves on a red ground looking most attractive and far more exciting than the standard Great Western colours which they carried for so many years.

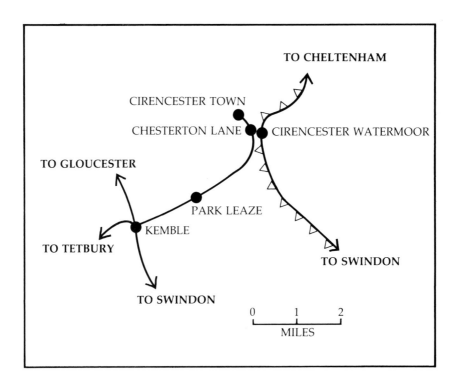

Kemble Junction. On the left, the 11.45 a.m. Paddington to Cheltenham is leaving. On the right, railbus W79975 works the 1.42 p.m. to Cirencester Town.

31.5.62   Author

The steam pumping-engine at Kemble. This raised water for the station, village and some of the Swindon Railway Works supply.

November 1966   S. Apperley

0–6–0PT No. 8779 works the 11.52 a.m. Kemble to Cirencester Town. Notice the piles of ballast.
2.6.54   Hugh Ballantyne

Railbus W79975 approaches Chesterton Lane Halt with the 3.05 p.m. Cirencester to Kemble. Part of the community it served can be seen in the background.
6.5.60   Author

The goods yard at Cirencester. The track is of bridge rail on longitudinal sleepers. Notice the large timber-built goods shed, centre. The locomotive coaling stage is immediately below the water tank, left.

c. 1900   GWR

This more distant view looking towards the terminus shows the station's position on the edge of the town. The engine shed is in the centre of the picture and the goods yard on the right, with the tall passenger station building beyond. In the right foreground is the pig dock which does not appear to have had much recent use. Access to the yard is via a rare and expensive type of switch – a diamond crossing with a double slip.

c. 1956   M.E.J. Deane

2–6–2T No. 4538 at Cirencester Town. A pannier tank stands outside the locomotive shed to the left of the signal-box, while in the right foreground are cattle pens.

c. 1955   M.E.J. Deane

A railbus stands at Cirencester Town station on a wet day. The tall station building was originally balanced by a train shed on its left.

c. 1962   Lens of Sutton

Railbus W79978 at Cirencester Town.

1960   M.G.D. Farr

Railbus at Cirencester Town, looking towards Kemble.

28.3.64   Author's Collection

Kemble to Tetbury

Although passengers and goods were conveyed by road between Tetbury Road station on the main Swindon to Gloucester line and Tetbury itself, first by carrier James Coventry and later by Joey Mills, this was only a stop-gap measure until a railway could be built to Tetbury. On 28 August 1872 Colonel Nigel Kingscote MP called a public meeting 'To consider the propriety of taking the necessary steps for obtaining railway communication between the Town of Tetbury and the Great Western Railway near Kemble Junction'. The GWR agreed to purchase fifty per cent of the shares if a company was set up, on condition that all the landowners assented to sell without litigation, all the land required for the railway. Although Miss Anna Gordon agreed to a railway crossing her estate from a junction at Tetbury Road, the idea of a junction with the main line at Kemble she found unacceptable. Undeterred, the Great Western continued negotiations with her, resulting in Kemble becoming a public station. An act authorizing the Tetbury branch from it was passed in 1884.

J. Harris & Co. of Brighton were the contractors appointed for building the line, the first sod being turned at Kemble on 18 October 1887. Construction was relatively easy and just over two years later the line was complete. Festivities began on the morning of 2 December 1889, the first public train being the 7.55 a.m. to Kemble. Traffic on the line received a boost when, four weeks later, a cattle market opened at Tetbury.

In 1926 the branch was used for the trials of a new type of locomotive which it was hoped would revolutionize the economy of rural lines. The Great Western obtained from the Sentinel Wagon Works two patent geared steam locomotives. A highly innovative machine, its boiler was vertical instead of horizontal and had its fire-box within, rather than at one end – in fact it looked like an enlarged contemporary domestic boiler. This vertical boiler was set inside, instead of outside, the cab. The mechanism was also set in a vertical position. Capable of a speed of 18 m.p.h., No. 12 was tested on Tetbury branch passenger trains, but unfortunately was not a success.

For real economies to be effected the line had to wait a further thirty-three years until the introduction of railbuses on 2 February 1959 – the same date as for the Cirencester branch. Although the Tetbury railbus increased traffic by as much as 150 per cent, the line closed on 6 April 1964, one of the last passengers being Mrs Butler, who had travelled on the first train seventy-five years earlier. The branch had already closed to freight in 1963.

A particularly busy time on the branch was at the end of each term when extra coaches were added to trains carrying pupil from Westonbirt Girls' School. The last school train ran just two days before closure when the 11.30 a.m. ex-Kemble and the 12.25 p.m. Tetbury to Kemble railbus was replaced by 0–6–0PT No. 1664 hauling two corridor coaches and a bogie luggage van.

The first station beyond Kemble was Jackaments Bridge Halt, opened in 1939 for the benefit of RAF personnel at Kemble aerodrome and closed in 1948. Beyond was

Rodmarton platform, opened in 1904. It was the first Great Western 'platform', a term borrowed by the company from Scotland where it had been in use before the end of the nineteenth century. Providing longer platforms than 'halts', they were usually staffed by senior grade porters who booked passengers, parcels and milk, whereas halts were generally unstaffed. Culkerton which had a timber building, latterly looking very derelict and used only by an average of forty passengers a month, was closed in 1956, but with the advent of railbuses, re-opened as an unstaffed halt. This new service also saw new rail-level halts opened at Churchs Hill and Trouble House, this latter being the only halt in the country just serving an inn.

The original station at Tetbury was constructed of timber so as to facilitate its removal if the line was extended, but as the fabric deteriorated it was reconstructed in brick in 1913, many of the original doors and windows being incorporated. In the 1930s the platform was lengthened to accommodate the strings of polo ponies brought by wealthy Indian Potentates to the Beaufort polo fields at Westonbirt. One interesting feature of the station drive was that it was situated in two counties.

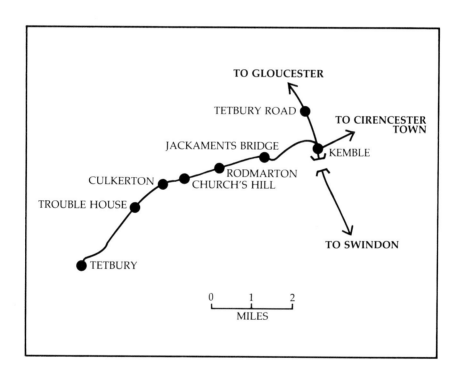

0–6–0PT No. 1658 (82C, Swindon) at Tetbury. The locomotive shed is to the left of the water tank.

c. 1955   M.E.J. Deane

Railbus W79977 at Tetbury having worked the 6.05 p.m. from Kemble.

31.5.62   Author

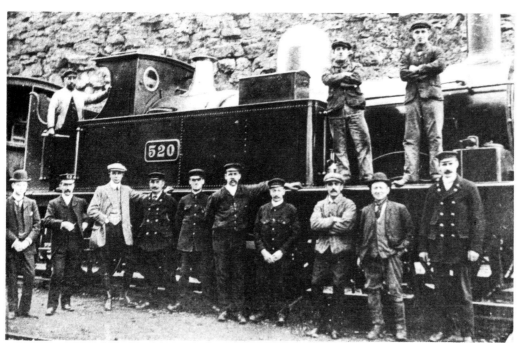

Staff gather round 517 class 0–4–2T No. 520 at Tetbury. The cliff north-east of the station looks stark; in later years it was shrouded by undergrowth .

c. 1905   Author's Collection

Cheltenham to Stow-on-the-Wold

The line between Cheltenham and Stow-on-the-Wold was part of the Banbury and Cheltenham Railway, a line built piece-meal. The first section of the line to be opened was a branch from Kingham, on the Oxford and Worcester line, to Chipping Norton. Then on 1 March 1862 a branch was opened from Kingham through Stow-on-the-Wold to Bourton-on-the-Water. Ten years later, the Banbury and Cheltenham Direct Railway was proposed, using the existing lines from Bourton to Chipping Norton and building a new branch from Cheltenham to Bourton and another onwards from Chipping Norton to a main line south of Banbury. It was originally envisaged that the main Cheltenham station would be in Leckhampton Road, but fortunately this plan was amended as having a station so far from the town centre would have discouraged passengers. Reason prevailed and trains used St James' as the terminus. The line from Cheltenham to Bourton-on-the-Water was opened on 1 June 1881 and the rest of the line through to Banbury on 6 April 1887. When the Midland and South Western Junction Railway was extended to Cheltenham on 1 August 1891, it had running powers over the single line between Andoversford and Cheltenham. This section of the line was doubled by the GWR in 1900 to combat the threat of a fourteen-mile extension which the MSWJR sought from Andoversford via Winchcombe, to a junction with the Midland Railway just south of Ashchurch station.

Between May 1906 and September 1939 the Banbury and Cheltenham Direct Railway was used by the unofficially named 'Ports to Ports' South Wales to Newcastle-upon-Tyne expresses'. These usually consisted of a six-coach corridor set with restaurant car. A through coach to and from Hull and Goole was attached and detached at Sheffield, adding two more ports. North Eastern and Great Western Railway coaches were used on alternate days. In May 1906 Leckhampton station had its name changed to Leckhampton and Cheltenham South (and was re-named Cheltenham and Leckhampton in April 1952) for the sole purpose of allowing the 'Ports to Ports Express' to pick up and set down at Cheltenham, for having to use the dead-end St James', with the need to couple another engine to the back to draw it onwards, would have proved time consuming and expensive. Even taking a direct route through Cheltenham it hardly lived up to being called an express: leaving Swansea at 7.40 a.m. it did not arrive at Newcastle until 6.32 p.m.

During both world wars the line proved a vital link, but with the development of road transport and the closure of ironstone mines at the north end of the line, traffic seriously declined. Cheltenham to Bourton-on-the-Water closed on 15 October 1962, the track being lifted three years later.

St James' station originally had two platform roads and two central carriage sidings, but was reconstructed in the early years of this century. An imposing, brick-built terminal station with a covered carriage approach fronting on St James' Square, it had two curved, semi-island platforms and two central carriage sidings. Signalling was arranged so that arrivals used the two northern platforms, but trains could depart from any road. The station closed to passengers on 3 January 1966.

South of St James' and Lansdown stations was a triangular junction where trains for Stow-on-the-Wold curved eastwards. Although through trains from Cheltenham to Paddington travelled via Gloucester and Swindon, the shortest, quickest and cheapest route from Cheltenham to London was not via Swindon, but over the Banbury and Cheltenham Direct Railway, changing trains at Kingham. Until it closed in 1927, a one-and-a-quarter mile long mineral line ran from Charlton Kings station to Leckhampton quarries and was worked by *Lightmoor*, a 0–4–0 tank engine built by Messrs. Peckett of Bristol. Beyond Charlton Kings, the main line continued its climb over the Cotswolds. The 192 yd long Woodbank viaduct consisted of twelve arches with a maximum height of 70 ft. The mortar, made from blue clay and ballast, set like iron; as the contractor discovered when he wished to take a few courses off the piers following a severe frost. He found the bricks and mortar impossible to separate. After the track had been lifted, the viaduct was blown up on 30 April 1967. Beyond was the 384 yd long Andoversford tunnel. Just before Notgrove station, the line passed through a cutting in solid rock at a summit of 760 ft above sea-level, which was claimed to be the highest of any GWR through route in England.

The station at Bourton-on-the-Water was originally a half-timbered construction with a two-tone tiled roof, but in the 1930s it was rebuilt in Cotswold stone with a stone-tiled roof, altogether an excellent design. The station at Stow-on-the Wold had a similar history, but had only one platform, whereas all the other stations, rather than halts on the line, had passing loops. The station was 475 ft above sea-level and a mile distant from the town, which was at a point nearly 300 ft higher.

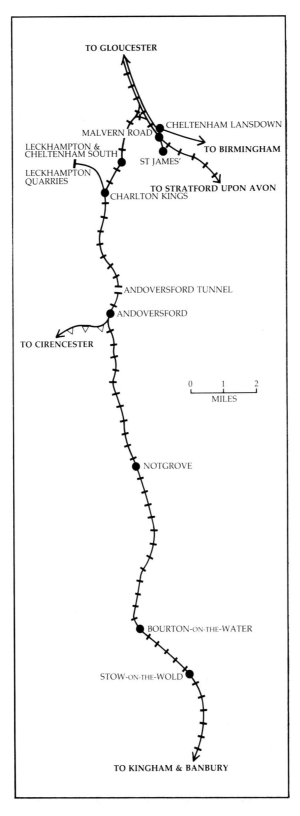

TO GLOUCESTER

CHELTENHAM LANSDOWN

MALVERN ROAD

TO BIRMINGHAM

LECKHAMPTON &
CHELTENHAM SOUTH

St JAMES'

LECKHAMPTON
QUARRIES

TO STRATFORD UPON AVON

CHARLTON KINGS

ANDOVERSFORD TUNNEL

ANDOVERSFORD

TO CIRENCESTER

0   1   2

MILES

NOTGROVE

BOURTON-ON-THE-WATER

STOW-ON-THE-WOLD

TO KINGHAM & BANBURY

2–6–2T No. 4116 arriving at Charlton Kings with the 11.18 a.m. Kingham to Cheltenham St James'.

27.2.60   Hugh Ballantyne

Dowdeswell viaduct, view towards Cheltenham.

21.4.65   Author

Type 4B inspection car at Notgrove. It seated two people and provided storage space behind for equipment. The 6 hp petrol engine drove a two-speed, two-direction gear box on the rear axle at a maximum speed of 25 m.p.h.

17.8.62   Author

The original station building at Bourton-on-the-Water, looking towards Kingham.

c. 1905   Lens of Sutton

2–6–2T No. 4100 at Bourton-on-the-Water with the 5.15 p.m. Kingham to Cheltenham.

17.8.62   Author

At Bourton-on-the-Water, 2–6–2T No. 5184 with the 10.58 a.m. Cheltenham to Kingham crossing the 11.18 a.m. from Kingham.

29.9.62   Hugh Ballantyne

The original single-line station at Stow-on-the-Wold, the signal-box was out of view to the left. This is the view towards Cheltenham. The keys are on the inside of the rails.

c. 1900   Author's Collection

The 1930s replacement station at Stow-on-the-Wold. Notice the tree growth since the upper photograph was taken. Between the closed signal-box and the station building is a corrugated iron goods shed. A shunter's pole leans against the signal-box window.

17.8.62   Author

Cirencester to Andoversford

The line between Cirencester and Andoversford was the remnant of a grandiose Manchester and Southampton Railway scheme of the 1840s. Financial problems caused the project to be dropped, but the idea of a line linking the Midlands with Southampton was not forgotten. In 1881 a railway was opened to give a direct route between Swindon and Southampton. Its promoters envisaged an extension from Swindon to the MR at Cheltenham, thus making it part of a through route, and it was through routes, rather than local lines, which paid their shareholders worthwhile dividends.

In 1881 the Swindon and Cheltenham Extension Railway was granted permission by parliament to construct a line from Swindon to the Banbury and Cheltenham Railway at Andoversford. However, the new company discovered to its chagrin that people were not exactly falling over themselves in their eagerness to invest, and a shortage of funds prevented the line being opened in its entirety. The section between Swindon and Cirencester was opened in December 1883 and six months later the railways south and north of Swindon were amalgamated to form the Midland and South Western Junction Railway. Funds eventually came in and work resumed. The main engineering task on the Cirencester to Andoversford section was the 491 yd long tunnel at Chedworth.

Construction was almost complete when at about four o'clock early on Monday morning 9 June 1890, a section of brickwork near the Chedworth end of the tunnel collapsed for a distance of 12 yd and a wedge of earth fell in, causing a hole to be formed on the slope of the hill above the tunnel. This alone would have been enough trouble, but in addition the contractor proved awkward. He refused to repair this damage, forcing the MSWJR to take legal action.

Early the following year restoration was complete and the line ready for inspection by the Board of Trade. However, the company was still not free from bad luck. About three weeks after inspection, and before the running powers over the Banbury and Cheltenham line had been agreed, a rapid thaw after a severe frost caused 120 yd of embankment at Chedworth to slip and this so damaged an underline bridge that it had to be rebuilt.

The line was ready for opening to goods traffic on 11 March 1891, when a heavy snowstorm blocked the line and it was not until the 16th of the month that a train carried railway officials from Andover to Cheltenham and the line was opened for freight. It was the custom to open a railway to goods traffic initially so that embankments could settle, and in any case, passenger traffic would have been held up until Cheltenham station had been sufficiently enlarged to take the extra trains.

In July 1891 the Midland Railway sent a telegram to the MSWJR: 'If you can arrange to work your engines without turning at Cheltenham, the rest of the work will be ready for opening on the first proximo'. There was now every hope that the impecunious company could become an important through route, be worked profitably and pass out of receivership. When E.T. Lawrence, the company secretary, met the newly appointed manager, Sam Fay, off the train at Cirencester in 1892 he said, 'Do you know this line is nearly bankrupt and there is not enough money in the bank to pay the staff at the end of the week?'. Fay replied, 'Don't say that, I see great possibilities in this line.' Although some weeks later the position was so bad that Fay himself had to go to various debtors to collect enough cash to pay the wages, eventually the line flourished to such an extent that the receiver was discharged in 1897. Between 1894 and 1898 Fay increased traffic receipts by 73 per cent for an increase in expenditure of only 18 per cent.

During both world wars the MSWJR proved invaluable, carrying military supplies to the channel ports and hospital trains from Southampton to the North. Drivers were sometimes so busy they did not see their families for a fortnight at a time, occasionally working twenty-four hours non-stop. On one occasion a doctor told a guard that the jerky efforts of a driver to climb the gradient of 1 in 75 between Foss Cross and Chedworth had thrown seven men off their stretchers.

Two mishaps occurred on this length of line. The first took place on 10 January 1901 when earth and rock fell in the cutting between Chedworth and Withington. The 2–4–0 tank engine No. 8 ran into it and was de-railed together with the first coach in which Mrs Purkess, the general manager's wife, happened to be travelling. Later the same year, a crash occurred when a contractor's trolley and a passenger train collided between Cirencester and Foss Cross.

The line from Andoversford to Cirencester, doubled in 1901, was singled in 1928 as an economy measure by the GWR which had taken over the MSWJR in 1923. Another economy was the closure the following year of the locomotive, carriage and wagon works at Cirencester. However, the real threat came in December 1958 when trains were diverted from Cheltenham (Lansdown) station, where they connected with trains from the North, to Cheltenham (St James'). This meant that the line could only deal with local passenger traffic and this was not sufficient to be economic. At the same time, the three express goods trains each way were withdrawn, leaving no regular goods trains between Andoversford and Cirencester. The final blow came in 1961 when it was announced that passenger traffic would be withdrawn from 9 September and the Cirencester to Andoversford section closed completely.

As the GWR would not permit the MSWJR to use Andoversford station until 1904, the company built its own at Dowdeswell, just south of the junction. When the track was doubled, the station site at Chedworth was needed for the extra line, and as there was insufficient room for platforms, a new station was built to the north. Although Foss Cross was in an isolated position, passengers came from Bibury and Coln Rogers and the station handled almost as much goods traffic as Cirencester. A nearby quarry supplied ballast for the whole of the MSWJR. During the Second World War one signalman kept rabbits under the floor of the waiting room until they were discovered by the authorities, who were opposed to this method of easing the food shortage!

The buildings at Cirencester were stone-faced as befitted one of the company's principal stations and a contrast to the red brick generally used elsewhere.

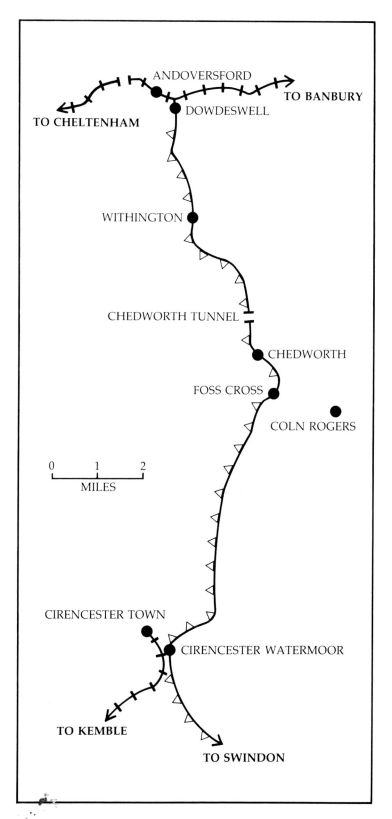

ANDOVERSFORD

TO BANBURY

DOWDESWELL

TO CHELTENHAM

WITHINGTON

CHEDWORTH TUNNEL

CHEDWORTH

FOSS CROSS

COLN ROGERS

0   1   2
MILES

CIRENCESTER TOWN

CIRENCESTER WATERMOOR

TO KEMBLE

TO SWINDON

A Midland & South Western Junction Railway loading gauge at Dowdeswell. To give it additional strength, a flat-bottom rail made by Messrs Krupp is to the left of the wooden post supporting it.
6.5.60   Author

MSWJR 0–6–0 No. 28 at the Midland Railway's Cheltenham Lansdown station. The curved brass plate on the centre splasher reads, 'Beyer, Peacock & Co. Ltd, Manchester, 1902'.

c. 1920   Author's Collection

The Railway Correspondence & Travel Society's 'East Midlander No. 2' Nottingham to Swindon rail tour passes Chedworth. Class 2P 4–4–0 No. 40489 (22B, Gloucester) piloted train engine of the same class No. 40454 (16A, Nottingham) from Cheltenham to Swindon works yard. At this date, an LMS engine on the MSWJR was a rarity.

6.5.56   Hugh Ballantyne

RCTS 'East Midlander No. 2' Nottingham to Swindon rail tour at Cirencester Watermoor. Class 2P 4–4–0 No. 40489 is piloting No. 40454 of the same class.

6.5.56   Lens of Sutton

U class 2–6–0 No. 31629 enters Cirencester Watermoor with a Southampton to Cheltenham Spa Lansdown express.

21.7.56   R.E. Toop

Southern Region U class 2–6–0 No. 31620 enters Cirencester Watermoor with the 1.56 p.m. Cheltenham Spa Lansdown to Southampton express.

21.7.56   R.E. Toop

Diesel railcar W19W at Gloucester Central forming a train to Ledbury.

16.5.59 R.E. Toop

W19W south of Barbers Bridge with the 1.25 p.m. Ledbury to Gloucester Central. Notice how near the ballast is to the boundary fence.

11.5.57 Hugh Ballantyne

The 6.24 p.m., the final passenger train from Gloucester Central to Ledbury, enters Barbers Bridge.

11.7.59   Hugh Ballantyne

The driver of 0–4–2T No. 1428 and a porter have a word at Newent. The train is running between Gloucester Central and Ledbury.

23.2.59   Author's Collection

The 6.24 p.m., the last train from Gloucester Central to Ledbury, calls at Newent. It is headed by 0–6–0 No. 3203 (85B, Gloucester).

11.7.59   Hugh Ballantyne

W19W calls at Newent with the 1.25 p.m. Ledbury to Gloucester Central.

16.5.59   R.E. Toop

W19W takes on passengers at Four Oaks Halt. The guard wears a smart white shirt and the boys have short trousers.

4.4.59   E. Wilmshurst

A Gloucester to Ledbury train arrives at Dymock while most of the staff gather on the other platform. A carriage drawn by two horses stands in the station yard. The platforms have been decorated with flower beds.

c. 1910   Author's Collection

W19W working the 5.25 p.m. Ledbury to Gloucester Central. Notice that glass in the canopy allows light on to the platform. The canopy brackets are also worthy of a second glance.

11.7.59 Hugh Ballantyne

An auto-train, worked by an unidentified 0–4–2T, arrives at Dymock. The engine is in the centre of the train. Most firemen disliked the engine being in the middle, as it meant that they never shared the companionship of their driver who was always in one of the control vestibules at the far end of each coach. Notice the gong which a driver in the vestibule could use to sound a warning.

c. 1954 M.E.J. Deane

The 6.24 p.m., the last 'Down' train from Gloucester Central to Ledbury, receiving a welcome at Greenway Halt. No. 3203 has gathered two wreaths. The coaches appear well-filled.

11.7.59   Hugh Ballantyne

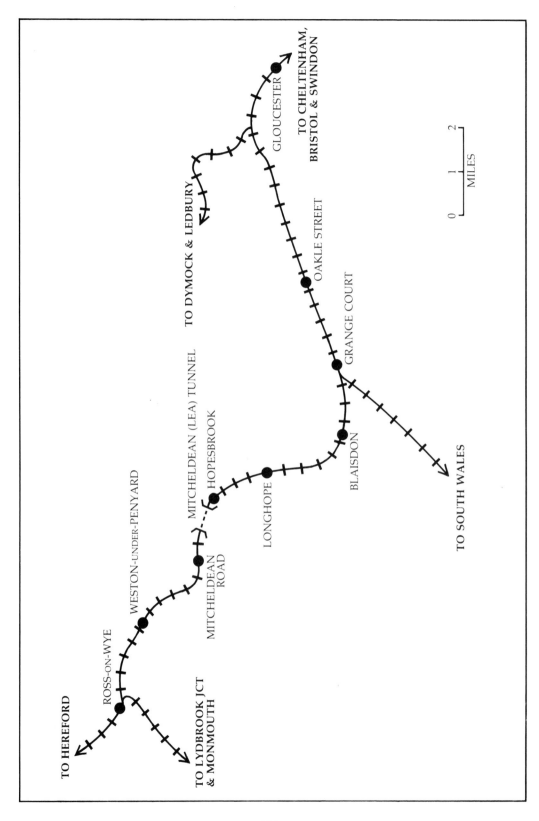

The unusually lengthy nameboard supported on posts made from old running rail.

1964   D. Payne

Grange Court to Longhope single-line electric token.

D. Payne

2–6–0 No. 7318 at Longhope with a Gloucester Central to Hereford train.

23.9.64   D. Payne

Leaving Longhope is 2–6–0 No. 7318. The siding in the foreground was taken out of use 1.7.64.
23.9.64   D. Payne

No. 7815 *Fritwell Manor* arriving at Longhope with a Hereford to Gloucester Central train.

23.9.64   D. Payne

At Newnham with the Steam Mills rail motor is 0–6–0ST. The bay platform was opened 4.8.07 especially for this service.

c. July 1907   Author's Collection

Ascending a gradient of 1 in 58 is 0–6–0PT No. 1623 with the 2.58 p.m. Newnham to Cinderford approaching Ruspidge Halt.

15.5.57   Hugh Ballantyne

With a 'Down' goods is 0–6–0PT No. 1627 near Ruspidge Halt.

24.4.62   Author

A 2021 class 0–6–0ST has yet to run round its train at Cinderford. The coaches probably belong to the Midland Railway. The yard appears very spacious. In the left foreground is a Thornycroft undertype steam lorry owned by Francis Wintle's Brewery, Mitcheldean. The building to the right of centre is a redbrick weighbridge house, while to its right are cattle pens.

c. 1905   Author's Collection

The 2.45 p.m. Cinderford to Newnham at Cinderford worked by No. 5408 (85B, Gloucester) and auto-car W206W. Until its conversion in 1933, No. 206 was formerly steam rail motor No. 86.

10.9.55   Hugh Ballantyne

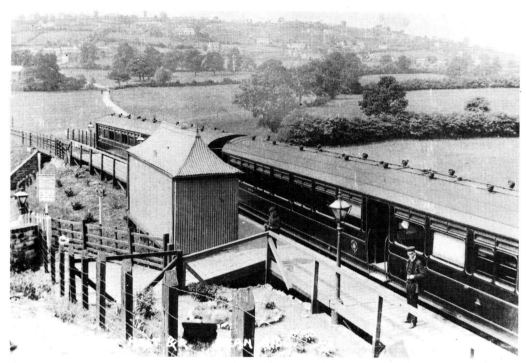

Auto-cars at the Drybrook Halt terminus.

c. 1910   Author's Collection

0–6–0ST No. 2113 with auto-car at Drybrook Halt. This is the view towards Newnham.

c. 1909   Author's Collection

Lydney to Coleford, Lydbrook Junction and Cinderford

Like the Bullo Pill to Cinderford line, the Lydney to Lydbrook Junction branch began life as a horse-worked plateway. Opened in early June 1810, it was principally used for the transport of Forest coal. In 1868 a broad gauge line was laid parallel with the tramroad between Wimberry Slade, near Speech House, opening on 19 April 1869 and converted to standard gauge three years later. This meant that some of the 3 ft 8 in gauge locomotives were converted to broad gauge and then altered to standard gauge. Not long after this, it was decided to upgrade the Milkwall tramroad to a railway and extend it to Coleford, the line from Coleford Junction being formally opened to passengers on 9 December 1875. One notable poster proclaimed: 'Success to the 7 and Y'. The Severn and Wye Railway was taken over in 1879 by the GWR and MR to become the Severn and Wye Joint Railway. At one time through services ran over the Severn Bridge from Berkeley Road to Lydbrook junction, with a connection at Parkend for Coleford. On 8 July 1929 trains from Berkeley Road terminated at Lydney Town, passenger trains through to Coleford and Lydbrook Junction being withdrawn. The Coleford branch was winding throughout most of its three and three-quarter mile length and was on a gradient of approximately 1 in 30. Freight services were withdrawn on 11 August 1967. Speech House Road to Coleford Junction closed on 12 August 1963, though the last train actually ran on the following day. Lydbrook Junction to Mierystock closed on 30 January 1956 and Mierystock sidings to Serridge Junction and Speech House Road on 21 November 1960, though a rail tour visited it on 13 May 1961.

It said much for the vigilance of the railway staff that with steam locomotives in close proximity to wooden station buildings, more did not catch fire. During the early hours of 20 July 1918, the timber-built Severn and Wye passenger station at Coleford went up in flames. Replaced with a brick building, it is interesting that passengers used an inadequate wooden station for forty-three years; a temporary station from 1919 until 1924 and a proper brick station for only five years before its closure in 1929.

Many of the sidings feeding the Lydney to Lydbrook Junction branch were on steep gradients and working instructions at some stations stipulated spragging the wheels of vehicles left on the main line. Between Lydney Junction and Lydney Town were three tracks – a rather unusual number. In addition to the 'Up' and 'Down' line, a bi-directional third track was laid on the site of the original tramway in 1889. Only used by goods and mineral trains, it carried trains in the 'Down' direction before 11 a.m., and after that hour, those in the 'Up'. The 187 yd long Lydbrook viaduct north of Lower Lydbrook station had a 5 m.p.h. speed restriction imposed. Unlike the practice of the big four main lines, the Severn and Wye Joint Railway retained red distant signal lights until 1945 when they were converted to the standard yellow colour. The line's joint nature was shown by the signal-boxes south of Parkend being of the MR type. Norchard

118

Colliery closed in 1957 and subsequently its site has been used by the Dean Forest Railway.

Lydney harbour, at one time important for shipping Forest coal, was served and owned by the tramroad. In post-Second World War years, a dwindling coal trade continued to Bristol, Combe Martin, Ilfracombe and Minehead and an annual trip made to the Scilly Isles. Eventually the Lower Docks branch was taken out of use on 18 November 1960, the Upper Docks branch following on 1 September 1963.

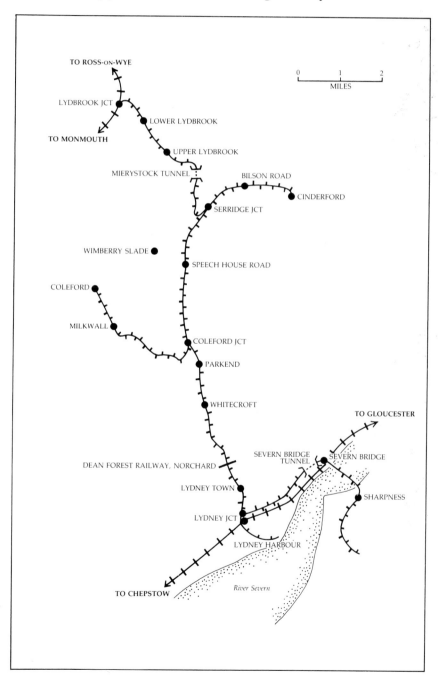

Contents of a Cannop colliery coal truck being tipped into sailing vessel at Lydney harbour. The wagon on the far right comes from Parkend colliery, and other wagons would also contain Forest coal.

c. 1905   Author's Collection

Lydney Junction, with the view towards Lydney Town from the footbridge connecting the Severn and Wye and the South Wales line platforms. On the right a passenger train headed by an 0–4–2T can be seen standing at the Severn and Wye platform (notice the MR style fence with sloping palings), the main South Wales line platforms being off the photograph to the left. In the middle distance is the locomotive shed, with the Steel Company of Wales', Lydney works beyond. To the left of the shed is the Permanent Way Department's crane.

c. 1955   M.E.J. Deane

0–6–0PT No. 1612 at Lydney Junction shed *c.* 1954. This was the Severn and Wye's main depot and the building behind the coaling platform was the repair shop. The grounded coach body on the left was provided in 1921 for the use of shedmen and cleaners. It cost £170 17s. 0d.

c. 1954   M.E.J. Deane

0–6–0PT No. 5417 (85B, Gloucester) at Lydney Town.

c. 1954   M.E.J. Deane

On the Dean Forest Railway, Norchard, an 0–6–0ST works a passenger train.

1.7.87   Author

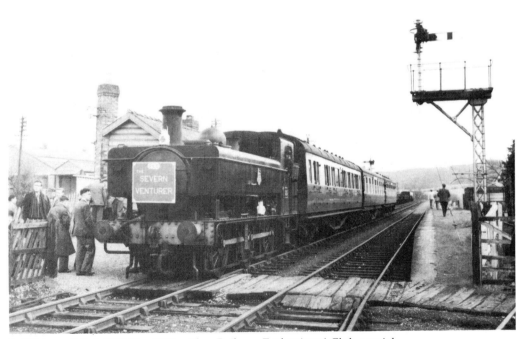

At Whitecroft 0–6–0PT No. 1625 with a Railway Enthusiasts' Club special.

15.4.56   Hugh Ballantyne

Ex-GWR diesel railcar W7 at the former Severn and Wye Coleford station with a Gloucestershire Railway Society's special. A water crane can be seen right, fed from the water tank on the far right. To the left of the railcar is the goods shed.

2.6.51   M.E.J. Deane

Hauling a track-lifting train, 0–6–0PT No. 1642 is watered at Serridge Junction. Firemen J. Needham is on top of the boiler, the guard is W. Robins, the driver R. Baldwin and T. Askew is the sub-inspector, Lydney Engineering Department.

24.6.60   Author's Collection

Empty wagons to collect lifted sleepers being pushed into Mierystock tunnel.

8.6.60   Author's Collection

Lydbrook viaduct, designed by George W. Keeling, engineer to the Severn and Wye Railway. The tallest masonry pier was 90 ft high. The speed of trains over the viaduct was limited to 5 m.p.h.

11.4.56   Author's Collection

Lydbrook Junction. Ex-GWR diesel railcar W7 working a Gloucestershire Railway Society special, stands on the branch to Serridge Junction, while an auto-train is on the Ross-on-Wye to Monmouth working.

2.6.51   Peter Davey

At Lydbrook junction is 0–4–2T No. 1445 and auto-car with the Ross-on-Wye to Monmouth train.
2.6.51   Peter Davey

0–4–2T No. 1401 (85B, Gloucester), of 'Titfield Thunderbolt' fame, approaches Lydbrook Junction with auto-car, working the 3.51 p.m. from Monmouth (Troy). 0–6–0PT No. 9619 pauses during shunting operations.

15.5.57   Hugh Ballantyne

Chepstow to Tintern Quarry

The Chepstow to Tintern Quarry line was part of the Chepstow to Monmouth branch. In the early 1830s boats operated a passenger service up the River Wye between Chepstow and Monmouth, but thirty years later, the need was felt for a faster form of transport. The outcome was the Wye Valley Railway which received its Act of Parliament in 1866. In due course Messrs Reed Brothers of London were given the contract and started work early in May 1874. Constructing the 1,190 yd long Tidenham tunnel through carboniferous limestone proved a hard task and was the line's most expensive feature. Boring night and day with the aid of the best machinery available, progress was only made at the rate of 2 yd a day, its completion taking almost two years. North of the tunnel was Shorn Cliff on which a shelf was cut for the railway, stone walls built above and below preventing landslips. The line opened on 1 November 1876, its only station in Gloucestershire being at Tidenham. Travellers were greeted by dramatic scenery as they emerged from the north portal of Tidenham tunnel on to a ledge of 150 ft above the Wye, and because of this the branch was acknowledged as being one of the most beautiful in the whole of the United Kingdom. They Wye Valley Railway was worked by the Great Western and, as with so many branch lines, it never really fulfilled the hopes of its promoters, consistently lost money, and was taken over by the GWR in 1905.

Passenger trains originally ran from Portskewett Pier, served by the ferry across the Severn, to Monmouth, but with the opening of the Severn Tunnel, from 1 December 1886 services were extended to and from Severn Tunnel Junction. From 1932 trains were based at Newport and from June 1939 the line saw GWR diesel railcars. It is interesting to record that it was on these railcars that BR diesel multiple units were based some twenty years later.

An unadvertised halt was opened at Tintern quarry on an unspecified date, and the public Netherhope Halt, close to the southern portal of Tidenham tunnel, on 16 May 1932. Due to the steep descent to Wye Valley Junction, all 'Down' goods trains were required to stop near Netherhope Halt to pin down wagon brakes so that the descent would be controlled.

By the late 1950s the branch was uneconomic, losing £13,000 annually. The last passenger service ran on 3 January 1959, the goods operation succumbing to the axe on 6 January 1964, though the line south of Tintern quarry remained open to work away ballast trains to various parts of the Western Region.

Tidenham had a low station building of limestone, similar in style to that which can still be seen at Tintern, though Tidenham had only a single platform. During the First World War Tidenham was closed between January 1917 and February 1918 as an economy measure and in 1928 the station was reduced to a halt status and its signal-box closed. Tidenham quarry, opened in the 1930s, progressively excavated Coombesbury Wood which is now entirely gone. Following the line's closure to passenger traffic, in March 1968 the station building was demolished by the quarry and its platform used as a

Tidenham (Dayhouse) quarry: 37235 draws empty wagons below the loading gantry. This is the view south.

12.7.83   Paul Strong

The driver watches from the rear cab as wagons pass below the loading gantry at Tidenham (Dayhouse) quarry. The platform in the foreground once belonged to Tidenham passenger station.
12.7.83   Paul Strong

Engine 37235 has now uncoupled from the loaded train at Tidenham quarry and will run round to the other end ready for the return journey – view south.

12.7.83   Paul Strong

after having been blocked for many years. Originally it had been used as a stable for ponies employed in the tunnel construction. Another interesting thing in the tunnel was that a gangers' cabin was hewn out of the 'Down' side approximately midway. There was a distant signal in the tunnel for 'Up' trains. It looked like a pair of spectacles. It was not on a post, but the gradient gave it height so that it could be seen from a distance.

LMS trains from Avonmouth tended to be loaded to the limit and it was not unknown for them to stall in the tunnel on the gradient of 1 in 64. Within its smoky confines, brakes had to be pinned down, and the first half of the train drawn to Clifton Down yard and then the rest collected. If a train was going very slowly and managed to reach the clapper, the driver thought it was worth persevering; but if it had not been reached, then division was the answer. If a driver had a heavy train and saw the Sea Mills distant 'on', he stopped there in preference to the home signal. This gave the advantage of starting downhill and being able to pick up speed in the dip at Sea Mills before reaching the bank, the guard ensuring that the couplings were kept taut on the descent in order to prevent chain snapping when the gradient rose.

The BPRP company was taken over jointly by the GWR and MR on 1 September 1890 when the GWR made a poor start. Its first train stalled at Horseshoe Bend and 'exclamations of the most forcible character rang out on the morning air in lusty chorus from the 468 working men passengers who were subject to this delay'.

The spur from Hotwells through the Avon Gorge to Sneyd Park Junction where the line from Clifton Down joined, was closed on 3 July 1922 in order that the Portway could be built and thus give improved road access to Avonmouth.

The extension line from Avonmouth along the bank of the Severn to Pilning was opened to goods on 5 February 1900. The line crossed the Severn Tunnel close to its eastern portal and, from a point midway between the later New Passage and Cross Hands Halts, followed the site of the Bristol and South Wales Union Railway. Excursion trains first used Severn Beach on 5 June 1922; it was opened permanently on 26 May 1924 and the passenger service extended to Pilning on 23 June 1928. In 1938 LMS trains worked through from the Midlands to Severn Beach. The line beyond Severn Beach closed to passengers on 23 November 1964 and to goods on 1 September 1968.

The railway was one of the main reasons why Avonmouth developed into an important port and one of its great features was the banana traffic. After devising a cooling system to preserve the fruit during the voyage from the West Indies, Fyffes imported the first commercial cargo (20,000 tons) in March 1901. Distribution for the fortnightly boats required 600 GWR banana vans being pre-heated during the winter months to 68 degrees F. At one time special boat trains were run for passengers. Three were required from Bristol and one from London in connection with the sailing of the *Royal Edward* on 12 May 1910, but latterly two or three coaches were attached to a Paddington to Bristol express and worked specially to Avonmouth. The last occasion when this occurred was 26 August 1964.

The Avonmouth to Filton line opened on 9 May 1910. During the First World War it gave access to large factories making war supplies and many of the workers travelled to and from the factories by rail. Between North Filton platform and the 302 yd long Charlton tunnel is an aircraft level crossing to give a taxi-ing-track from the erecting hangar to a runway. Originally opened in 1947 for use by the Brabazon, the crossing is still used intermittently. The line closed to regular passenger traffic on 23 November 1964, but until 9 May 1986 one train served North Filton Halt morning and evening.

Excursion trains were run to Clifton Down station not far from Clifton Zoo, and these 'monkey specials' proved very popular, especially those from South Wales, until the opening of the Severn road bridge in 1966 which caused these to decline by 54 per cent. They ran midweek every Tuesday, Wednesday and Thursday from the end of May until the end of August. A chord line, opened in 1970 between Patchway junction and Filton West Junction, avoided the need for a locomotive to run round its train at Stoke Gifford or Stapleton Road.

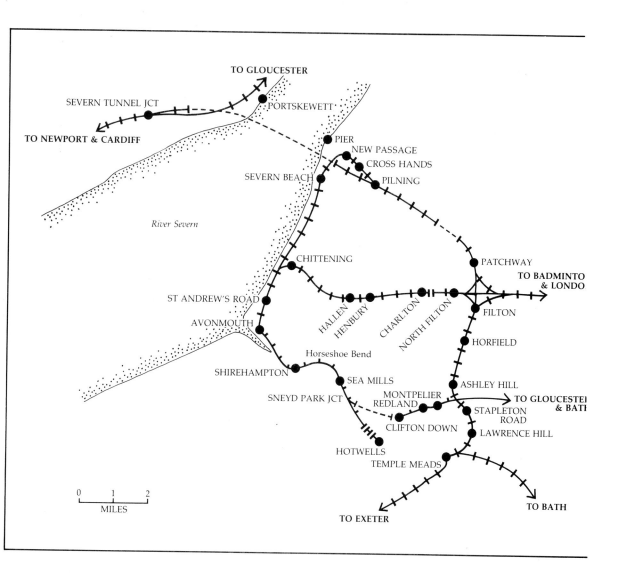

An ex-GWR 0–6–0 shunting coal wagons at Clifton Down, a station which dealt with a considerable tonnage of this commodity.

c. 1950   M.E.J. Deane

Two passenger trains stand head-to-tail at Clifton Down. The nearest train consists of four-wheeled coaches hauled by an open-backed 0–6–0ST. Notice the ridge and furrow roofs sheltering both platforms, and the substantial station building, making the ivy-covered signal-box appear tiny. To the right, some coal wagons can be seen in the yard.

c. 1905   M.J. Tozer Collection

Diesel hydraulic locomotive D7001 with a steam crane, lifting rail at Sea Mills. The style of fence indicated the line's association with the Midland Railway.

4.4.65   M.G.D. Farr

The Royal train at Avonmouth for the opening of the Royal Edward docks. The GWR 0–6–0ST has the correct headcode – a lamp on each iron. The Royal coat-of-arms is mounted on the centre splasher and the buffers are carefully burnished.

9.7.08   Author's Collection

The signalman at Hallen Marsh collecting the single-line tablet from the driver of DMU W55032. The reflection can be seen in the coach window on the right.

25.7.74 Author

A collision on the single line between Severn Beach and St Andrew's Road. Snow lies on the ground.

Early 1947 Author's Collection

DMU W50861 at Severn Beach working the 2.00 p.m. Severn Beach to Bristol Temple Meads. The station was unusual for two reasons: there was no shelter on the platform, and the office buildings were at right angles to the track.

3.6.63   Author

A DMU with power cars W51319/W51304 leaving North Filton platform with the 4.45 p.m. to Temple Meads. Used by workers, the halt had only two trains daily; an arrival in the morning and a departure in the afternoon.

21.8.80   Author

Severn tunnel pumping station. Coal for the engines was taken along the rather overgrown siding in the centre.

31.10.58   Author

People pose around a train at Hotwells station. The base of the train's headlamp fitted into a spigot at the front of the engine. The station was set in a cramped position between the cliff on the left and the river beyond the wall on the right.

1895   Author's Collection

An 0–4–2T climbs towards Clifton Down tunnel from Sneyd Park Junction.
c. 1900   Author's Collection

The opening of the Bristol and South Wales Union Railway and ferry, the train running to the end of the pier. New Passage Hotel stands at the landward end of the pier.
25.8.1863   Courtesy of *The Illustrated London News*

Fairford Branch

Although the Fairford branch had four miles of its track in Gloucestershire, it looked towards Oxford. The first proposals for building it were made in 1836 when a rail link was planned between Cheltenham and London. These particular schemes were thwarted, but in 1861 a line was opened from Yarnton, just north of Oxford, to Witney. In October that year, Cheltenham residents planned the East Gloucestershire Railway (EGR) linking their town with Witney. It was anticipated that the Midland Railway would work the EGR, but the GWR disputed the Midland's right to do so and, following Board of Trade arbitration, the Great Western's view was upheld.

The first sod was cut in a field near Cheltenham by Lady Russell, the chairman's wife, on 31 March 1865. After using the silver shovel to throw the turf into a wheelbarrow, she beat a hasty retreat before a large, unruly crowd. Shortage of funds eventually stopped work, though later the Stow-on-the-Wold branch used some of the earthworks, including Dowdeswell tunnel. As the Witney to Fairford section was over level country where the minimum of earthworks was required, it was decided to construct this portion first. Eventually the poverty-stricken EGR managed to discover a contractor willing to take a large number of shares in lieu of payment and work started in May 1869. Early the following year construction stopped as the company was quite unable to pay even the small amount to its contractor. Work resumed in the autumn when the EGR signed an agreement with the GWR for the latter to work the line in return for 50 per cent of the gross receipts. This 14 mile long extension opened on 15 January 1873.

It was still hoped that the line would reach Cheltenham, or even Cirencester only nine miles beyond Fairford, but the GWR was unwilling to give support and the necessary cash could not be raised. The Witney Railway and the EGR were both absorbed by the GWR on 1 July 1890.

In 1906 the branch was the first single line on the GWR to be equipped for Automatic Train Control working, which meant that a driver would receive an audible warning if he passed a signal at danger. Previous experiments had been on double track and the system required modification for use on a single line. So successful was it that every distant signal between Yarnton junction and Fairford was abolished and replaced by an ATC ramp.

By 1962 only about a dozen passengers used the station daily. The line was clearly uneconomic and so closed completely on 10 August 1962, track being lifted two years later.

Fairford station, situated about three-quarters of a mile from the town, had the appearance of a through, rather than terminal, station, in order that the line could have been extended easily without having to rebuild it. Two engines were allocated to the timber-built shed at Fairford. These were crewed by four drivers and four firemen, while two cleaners worked on the night shift. The first footplate crew booked on at 5.30 a.m., pumped water into the tank and took the first passenger train to Oxford. The second set of men booked on at 8 a.m. and pumped more water before leaving with the next passenger train which also collected full milk churns from the various branch-line stations. The third crew booked on at 1.20 p.m. and was responsible for the 2.12 p.m. passenger to Oxford. The fourth set of men came on duty at 4.05 p.m. when they shunted the afternoon goods.

Until 1940 Lechlade had only a single platform and a looped siding, but wartime traffic made it necessary for another siding to be laid and the loop extended. The new siding was laid on the site of a former line lifted early this century, which had served a ballast pit. Lechlade station was frequented by such famous people as William Morris, Dante Gabriel Rossetti and other Pre-Raphaelites.

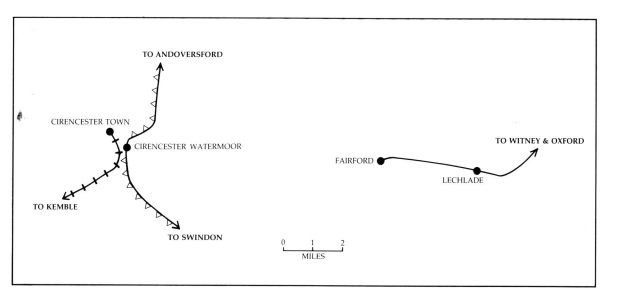

At Fairford 0–6–0PT No. 7411, still in green livery with GWR lettering, works the 2.02 p.m. to Oxford. The train is composed of corridor coach stock.

2.6.54   Hugh Ballantyne

On a dull day, 0–6–0 No. 2221 stands outside the timber-built Fairford engine shed. Right, a grounded horse-box serves as a locomen's cabin. Outside a driver is repairing a puncture to his bicycle, while his fireman, perhaps the owner of the motor cycle, looks on. At one time it was hoped that the line on which the vans are stabled would have been extended to Cirencester.

2.7.60   Author

Fairford, the view towards the stop blocks. By the 'mushroom' water tank is 0–6–0PT No. 7404, and 0–6–0 No. 2221 is outside the timber-built locomotive shed. The concrete post, right, was designed so that a Tilley lamp could be hoisted at night.

2.7.60   Author

0–6–0 PT No. 3653 at Fairford with a train for Oxford.

c. 1953   M.E.J. Deane

A young lad looks out of the cab of 0–6–0 PT No. 4676 beside the goods shed at Fairford.

c. 1953   M.E.J. Deane